Patent Constructions

NEW

Architecture

made

in Catalonia

Edited by Albert Ferré

The German Architecture Museum (Deutsches Architekturmuseum, DAM) is pleased to cooperate once again this year with the Frankfurt Book Fair and its programme of specific themes and guests of honour. This cooperation is now a tradition dating back to 1995, year in which, in collaboration with the Architecture Centre Vienna, the DAM organized a large exhibition covering the vast range of 20th-century Austrian architecture. Our contributions to the Book Fair's cultural programme continued with Ireland, Portugal, Switzerland, Greece, the Arab world and Korea. We are now planning a joint project with Turkish partners for the 2008 Book Fair.

In keeping with all of the above, we are very happy to offer the DAM's services and premises for a temporary exhibition on Catalan architecture. We thank the publisher ACTAR for the conception and realization of the exhibition and catalogue. We are especially grateful to the Institut Ramon Llull (IRL), the Catalan Institute of Culture, without whose generous funding this addition to the Book Fair would not have been possible.

Alongside this regional theme, the DAM is also holding the Mies van der Rohe Foundation's 2007 European Union Prize for Contemporary Architecture and the exhibition Gaudí Unseen (also with the support of the IRL) about works to complete Antoni Gaudí's Sagrada Família church. The present exhibition, Patent Constructions: New Architecture Made in Catalonia, is therefore contextualized in two ways: as an extension of the innovative and productive local tradition and as part of the cultural diversity of unified Europe. Thus it gives the visitor insights which are both inspiring and surprising. There is another aspect which is perhaps worth mentioning here: Patent Constructions is the second time that the DAM has focused on Catalan architecture. In 1991, in the run-up to the 1992 Barcelona Olympic Games, we showed a series of outstanding projects from the city. Accordingly, in our own way, we continue to help boost the robust creative force of architecture in Catalonia and the acceptance of that role there.

Peter Cachola Schmal and Annette Becker
Deutsches Architekturmuseum

Architecture draws on areas of knowledge as wide ranging as aesthetics, urban economics, art history and physics. This generalist condition alone of a profession spanning several disciplines and combining technology, thought and creativity, which has led it play a fundamental role in the building of cities and the development of civilizations, would justify fully organizing an architecture exhibition within a programme which seeks to be the showcase of the cultural activity of a territory. If this territory is Catalonia, the exhibition is especially pertinent.

The architecture produced in Catalonia has often been in the vanguard of Europe, especially so in the period from the return to democratic government in the late 1970s to the hosting of the Olympic Games in 1992, a time in which our country went through a new stage aimed at the restructuring and development of our cities, above all in the definition of the public space. But since then new and different social needs have emerged, and the rapid process of technological change in all areas of production and knowledge due to the need for constant innovation and growing specialization has become routine. How does Catalan architecture respond to this new demands, what contributions does it make to the advancement of our society?

The activities, as a whole, organized by the Institut Ramon Llull for the debut of Catalan culture at the 2007 Frankfurt Book Fair gave us the chance to answer that question, and to do so in front of an international, specialized public who will appraise critically our answers. This would not have been possible without the collaboration of the Deutsches Architekturmuseum, co-producer of the exhibition, and the curatorship of Actar. We trust that the answers we present here will contribute to confirming the never-ending need for a socially useful and propositive architecture.

Josep Bargalló
Director of the Institut Ramon Llull

INDEX

PATENT CONSTRUCTIONS
New Architecture Made in Catalonia

Architecture once drove the technological progress of civilization: The construction of Gothic cathedrals or of Brunelleschi's dome were historical milestones comparable, for example, to the decoding of the human genome today. It is obvious that architecture has long lost this pioneering, vanguard role, and nowadays is usually regarded as a service industry where innovation and inventiveness become undesired risk factors, obstacles to the correct implementation of a project. Under this view, the architect is now expected to act either as an art director or as the supervisor and manager of the building process. Whereas innovation is increasingly valued by our knowledge society and our global economy as the fundamental asset of any industry, architecture gets paradoxically stuck in the rejection of all experimentation and the subsequent inertia of repetition.

This book looks for exceptions, and testifies to Catalonia's ongoing potential as a centre of architectural innovation. Here, the combination of professional vision, craftsmanship and industrial expertise in a society traditionally receptive to formal experiments allows for the inventive transformation and improvement of the living environment. From this perspective, architecture is detached from its supposed and oft-vindicated artistic status, and is presented again as a useful and productive system of knowledge, the joint endeavour of a network of thinkers and doers.

This is a book on products as well as on the buildings and environments for which they were conceived. The products are attempts to solve specific program requirements, new social demands, environmental needs, budget limitations and design aspirations to improve on the status quo. They are proving grounds of architectural innovation.

Organised in four thematic sections corresponding to different scales and priorities of the innovation—structure, skin, habitat and landscape—the exhibition is an itinerary through programmatic, spatial and technical innovations produced by architects practicing in Catalonia over the last five years. Often of a low-tech nature, conceived and built with small budgets, these innovations do not originate in research centres, under comprehensive investment plans, with the resources typical of other technological industries, but must rely on personal inventiveness, personal ambition, and the ability to build personal relationships.

Although the thirty featured products—ranging from blind systems to urban spaces—were designed and produced in and for a particular context, with specific requirements and limitations, the value of the innovation lies in their ability to be applied to other situations. Together, these products and experiences form an export catalogue of new architectural solutions, in which the protagonists are not the buildings themselves, but fragments of them, prototypes and patents. If there is a way in which personal experimentation finds its way to broader markets, it is in the form of patented ideas.

Albert Ferré, Jaime Salazar, Ricardo Deves

STRUCTURE

ACTIVE ROOF
Hybgrid: Structural adaptable system (2002-2009)

Promotor Sistemes i Estructures de Geometria Variable, SCP (SEGV)
Proyecto subvencionado por CIDEM-Generalitat de Catalunya, Arts and Humanities
Research Council of England, Scottish Arts Council
Architects HYBRIDa: Silvia Felipe, Jordi Truco
Project team Marco Verde, Emmanuel Rufo Calderón González, Giacommo Venditti
Control engineering Ecomunicat
Contract management Hybridworks
Project management HYBRIDa
Management consultants Trampolí Tecnològic de Girona
Material consultants Centre for Biomimetics, University of Reading
Structural consultants Buro Happold: Wolf Mangelsdorf
Legal consultants ZBM Patents
Budget Prototype: € 30.000 / Pilot test: € 600.000 / Building: € 2.000.000
Photographs Sue Barr, HYBRIDa

The purpose of this project was to design a process-system capable of generating multiple undetermined forms according to required spatial needs. We worked with the design of a physical system (**phenotype**), capable of articulating in different configurations, as well as in the design of a digital process (**genotype**) that allows us to go from the multiple spatial needs to their formalization.

Phenotype: the physical system bases its formal articulation on the property of elastic deformation. The system grounds its behavior on the elastic properties and the continuity of materials like polymers or compounds (in the latter, the conjunction of the resistant capacity with elastic capacity is optimum). This physical system is organized on a grid made up of strips of three layers of compound material. These strips are continuous and performed to acquire inertia without the need to submit the material to unnecessary internal tension before receiving structural loads.

The whole can generate formal and structural differentiation (inertia) due to the modification of relative distances between these strips. The modification of these distances instantly provokes a change of curvature in the system. These distances are easily modified because of the presence of certain elements that we call actuators. These are located between strips and take on four positions. The modification of the local position of each actuator provokes an effect of modification of the global shape of the whole of the system.

Genotype: programmatic and spatial needs are transferred to the phenotype through parametric control. The system design works with software where limits, properties, and possibilities that the physical system allows are entered. The program calculates and transmits the parametric information to a database, which immediately communicates the local position to each actuator.

We designed a general and complex system, capable of adapting to multiple requirements by means of extremely simple laws. The system is the catalyst of information coming from such diverse disciplines as architectural design, materials engineering, computer programming, and structural engineering. The final form of the artefact is no longer the product of the personal and unidirectional vision of the architect, but it is directly informed by the system that makes it possible.

2.2.0 Morphing capacity by elastic deformation

2.2.0.1 Scheme of Actuator / Curvature ratios

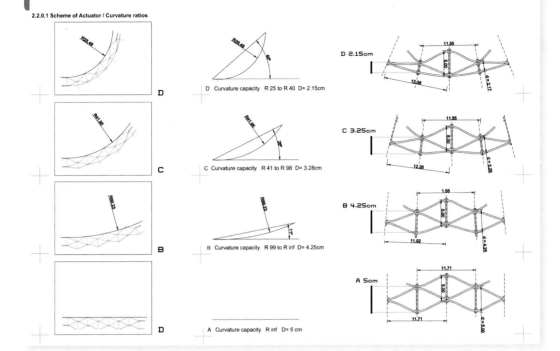

D 2.15cm

C 3.25cm

B 4.25cm

A 5cm

D Curvature capacity R 25 to R 40 D= 2.15cm

C Curvature capacity R 41 to R 98 D= 3.28cm

B Curvature capacity R 99 to R inf D= 4.25cm

A Curvature capacity R inf D= 5 cm

2.2.1 Defining the actuators

In this graphics we can appreciate the relation between some particular curve and the length of the actuators to achieve it (always this association must be done for a certain specific scale).
We start labeling the actuators (screws) according to this relation length. All the local positions of the actuators will have a direct repercussion in the global shape.
We have synthesized the lengths in four positions; each position will have a letter A, B, C or D, and each letter will correspond to a curvature radius. Later on we will analyze 3d shapes ,we will find their sections and we will use the system to reproduce them in a physical model.
the analysis must be really thoroughly done, because the final shape absolutely depends on this precision.

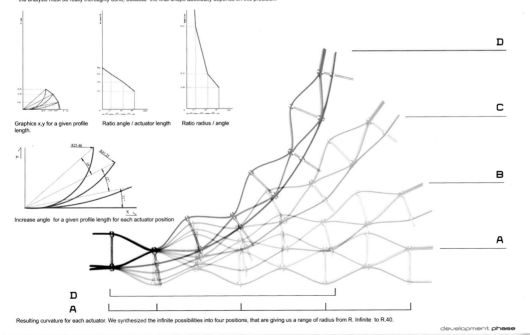

Graphics x,y for a given profile length.

Ratio angle / actuator length

Ratio radius / angle

Increase angle for a given profile length for each actuator position

Resulting curvature for each actuator. We synthesized the infinite possibilities into four positions, that are giving us a range of radius from R. Infinite to R.40.

development phase

3.1.0 Designing the digital process. The genotype

3.1.1 Parametric morphological manipulation toolbar

spatialconfiguration 01

sphere modifier 01
radii...............................(R100, R2100)
location...................................(11, 40, 5)
sphere modifier 02
radii...............................(R140, R2150)
location...................................(39, 40, 5)
sphere modifier 03
radii...............................(R140, R2100)
location...................................(26, 80, 5)

This toolbar sets the link between the abstract programmatic and spatial necessities and the materialization of the artifact. These requirements are digitally shaped by means of the parametric manipulation of, what we have called, **Sphere Modifiers** (in the toolbar "Sphere"). The user can activate each of them and set the value of its two defining radii as well as the coordinate position of its center.

The parameter of max. and min. radii have been previously calculated by the plug-in, when the user was required to define the size of the **Member Length**. There is a scale relation between this local size and the maximum and minimum curvature radii that the system is able to achieve.

3.1.2 Morphological simulation toolbar

Calculates the previous inputs and gives a digital visualization of the 3D shape informed by the Sphere Modifiers.

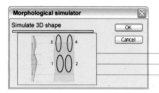

spatialconfiguration 02

sphere modifier 01
radii...............................(R100, R2100)
location...................................(25, 34, 5)
sphere modifier 02
radii...............................(R100, R2100)
location...................................(79, 10, 5)
sphere modifier 03
radii...............................(R100, R2120)
location...................................(79, 40, 5)

spatialconfiguration 03

sphere modifier 01
radii...............................(R150, R260)
location...................................(16, 43, 5)
sphere modifier 02
radii...............................(R150, R260)
location...................................(34, 43, 5)
sphere modifier 03
radii...............................(R140, R260)
location...................................(16, 81, 5)
sphere modifier 04
radii...............................(R140, R260)
location...................................(34, 81, 5)

3.1.3 Analysis of the curvature sections and parametric definition of actuators

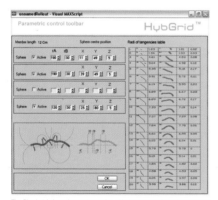

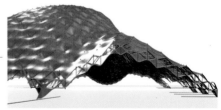

spatialconfiguration 01

The Plug-in labels each curvature radius with the amount of members and the required actuator position.

3.1.4 Physical actuators data transferring toolbar

Link with the material artifact. Transfers the actuator labels to those in phenotype.

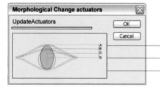

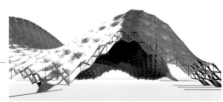

spatialconfiguration 02

spatialconfiguration 03   Project phase

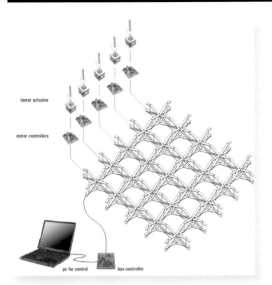

linear actuator

motor controllers

pc for control   bus controller

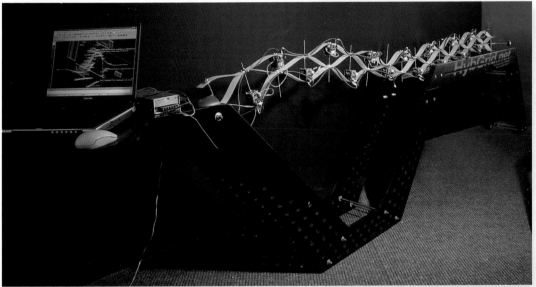

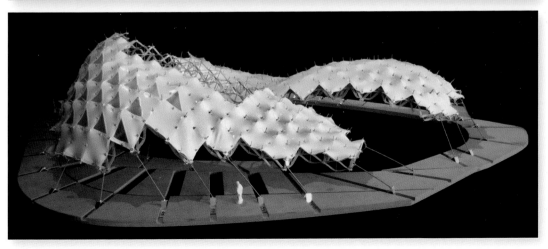

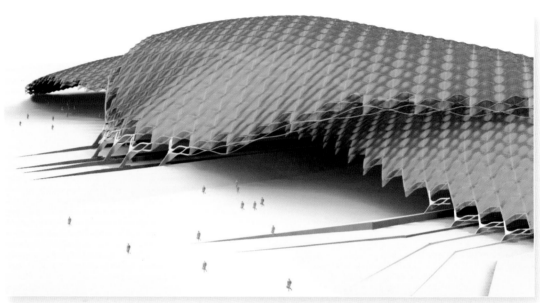

MALLEABLE STRUCTURE
5 Senses lounge bar (2005-2006)

Location Empuriabrava, Castelló d'Empúries
Client Evaristo Gallego / Gallego World
Architects Jordi Fernández, Eduardo Gutiérrez (ON-A) | www.on-a-lab.com
Technical architect Xavier Badia
M&E engineering Javier Escribano/Professional Assistent
Contractor Construccions Joan Fusté
Glass installation Vidres Gracia, Josep Ponsati
Laminated glass Cricursa
Steel cut and folding Laser Goded
Steel construction CMTPSL
Air conditioning Aiterm
Paint Talyali
Floors Quimpres
Carpentry Fusteria Gironella
Furniture Ergodec, Euromoble, Ramon Pujades, Fredterm

Lighting CA2L
Acrylic glass Complas
Vinyl Retolam
Sound Pentamusic
Model Guillermo Beluzo, Marcelo Cortez
Floor area 215 m²
Photographs Lluís Ros, ON-A

Empuriabrava is a development of vacation homes that is only completely full in the summer. The project takes up the ground level of an existing building located in a group of homes that attempts to don the character of a traditional village.

The inspiration for the configuration of the premises and of its subdivision into more intimate spaces was the image of a bone cell, characterized by its numerous separated adjoining cavities of one material that forms "walls" and "roofs." Steel was the material that would allow us to generate this type of space. We created an irregular, deformed, stretched and molded three-dimensional mesh to adapt to the existing architecture of the building and to generate the spaces required for the program. This mesh is made up of nearly 400 laser-cut and creased pieces of steel with a thickness of 3 mm, which form that perforated "bone tissue." This variety of different spaces, connections and configurations, make each perspective unique, each reflection and each shade of light different.

The view from the outside is characterized by the three-dimensional mesh, painted white, that emerges from the existing building and whose empty spaces are covered in blue-toned glass. On the inside, black is used for every element other than the mesh: The service box, the sound insulating material, the facilities, the spotlights, the furniture, the floor... Each of these elements has a particular function but at the same time blends into a black whole to highlight the presence of the white structural steel mesh.

At night, from the outside, the bar is a bizarre lamp of varying colors while during the day, it is an intense blue volume with irregular facets.

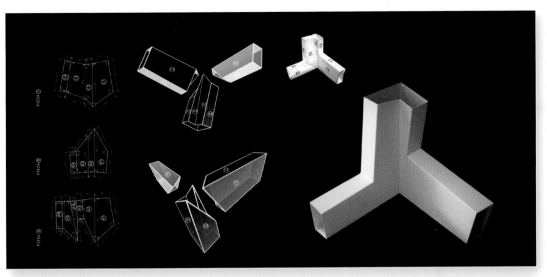

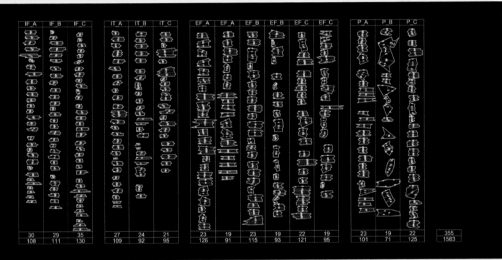

IF A	IF B	IF C	IT A	IT B	IT C	EF A	EF A	EF B	EF B	EF C	EF C	P A	P B	P C	
30	29	35	27	24	21	23	19	23	19	22	19	23	19	22	355
108	111	130	109	92	95	126	91	115	93	121	95	101	71	125	1583

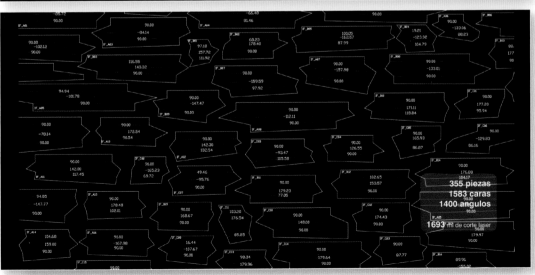

355 piezas
1583 caras
1400 ángulos

1693 ml de corte laser

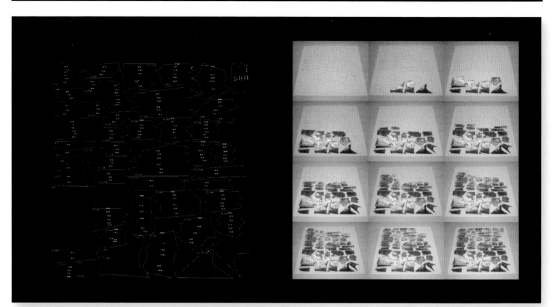

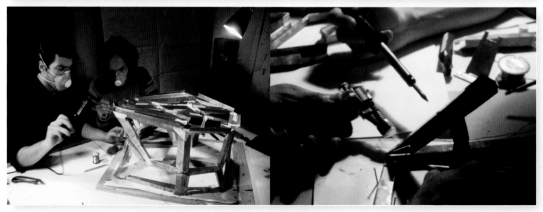

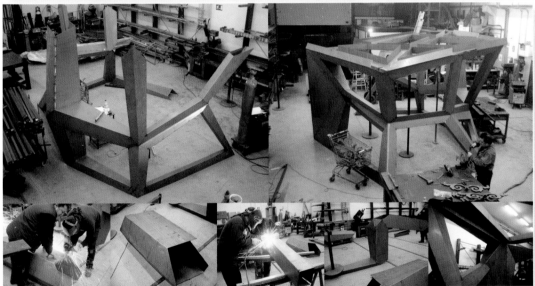

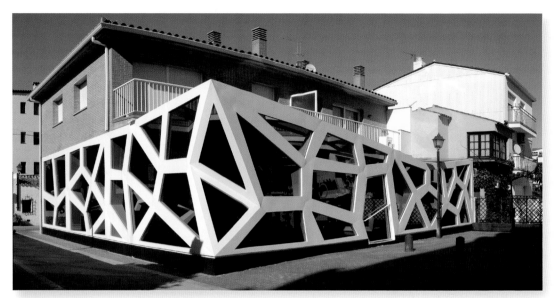

COMBINATORY POLES
Shading and lighting system
for three urban parks (1997-2006)

Location Jardins de Fabra & Coats, Sant Andreu, Barcelona (A3a); Plaça Pius XII, Gran Via, Sant Adrià de Besòs (A3b); Plaça Nicaragua, Barri de Sant Joan, Montcada i Reixac (A3c)

Client Ajuntament de Barcelona (A3a); Ajuntament de Sant Adrià de Besòs (A3b); Mancomunitat de Municipis de l'Àrea Metropolitana de Barcelona, Ajuntament de Montcada i Reixac (A3c)

Architects Eva Prats, Ricardo Flores

Design team Frank Stahl, Cristina Treviño, Paola Vallini, Antonella Sgobba (A3a); Eugenia Troncoso, Hernán Barbalace, Cinzia De Luca, Niels Toft, Mads Boserup (A3b); Andrea Schneider, Constanza Chara, Paula Fernandez, Laura Geraci, Fotini Trigonaki (A3c)

Models Fabián Asunción, Soledad Revuelto, Frank Stahl, Armin Schmidt (A3a); Israel Hernando, Angela Wright, Aljona Lissek, Tanja Dietsch (A3b); Angela Wright, Ellen Barten, Nadia Mustopo, Andrea Schneider, Horacio Arias (A3c)

Structural engineering Manuel Arguijo

Landscape engineer Mònica Martí

Contractor COSERSA, Emilio Comino, José María Benach (A3c)

Total area 4.680 m² (A3a); 7.200 m² (A3b); 2.931 m² (A3c)

Photographs Giovanni Zanzi, Ester Rovira, Álex García (A3a); Álex García, Jordi Bernadó (A3b); Álex García, Jonny Pugh (A3c)

The work with standard lamp post profiles began with the project of the gardens of Fabra & Coats, where we had proposed a pergola-like structure where climbing plants could grow on. The engineer's calculations proposed using round tubes with continuous cross-sections and additional reinforcing plates when the pergola became too high. The drawing adopted a disproportionate dimension which radically changed the intention and the initial image of the design. We needed another solution.

We constantly see standard posts holding up stoplights or electric lighting on streets. These elements are quite thin compared to the length and the branching out they tend to have. Their tapered cross section make them thicker towards the ground and continuously reduces them towards the sky. This quality, which we could call a plant-like quality, seemed an advantage to using them as a base to design other urban elements with — elements which required a slender profile, capable of camouflaging itself and disappearing into the urban context.

Since we were dealing with standard industrial pieces, their initial price was very low and although we had to add the cost of the metalwork, the final price was very competitive. This allowed us to use them in several situations:

1. Gardens of Fabra & Coats. Circular posts to create a romantic tunnel, an urban garden that needed a certain thickness of greenery before the surrounding wall.
2. Plaça de Pius XII. Lower the steps in front of a huge building, a forest-pergola that provides continuous vegetation and flowers.
3. Plaça de Nicaragua. Bird-lights that look towards the river park of the Besòs.

A3a. Gardens of Fabra & Coats (1997-1999)

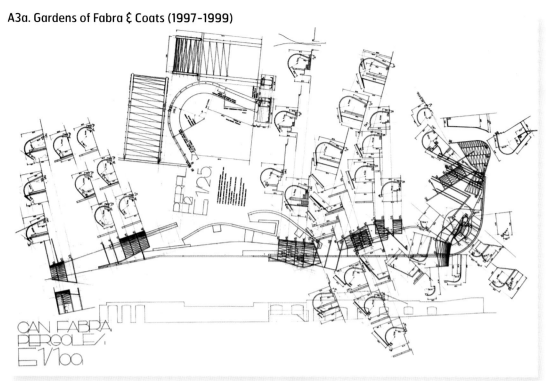

A3b. Plaça de Pius XII (2001-2004)

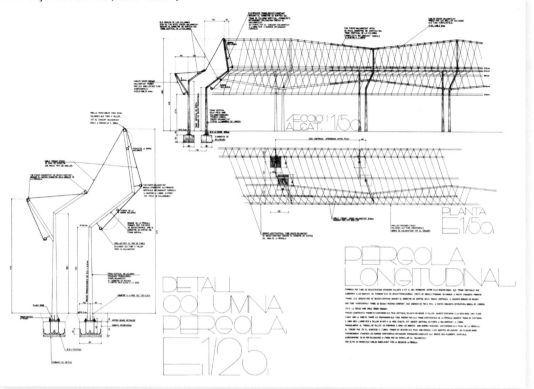

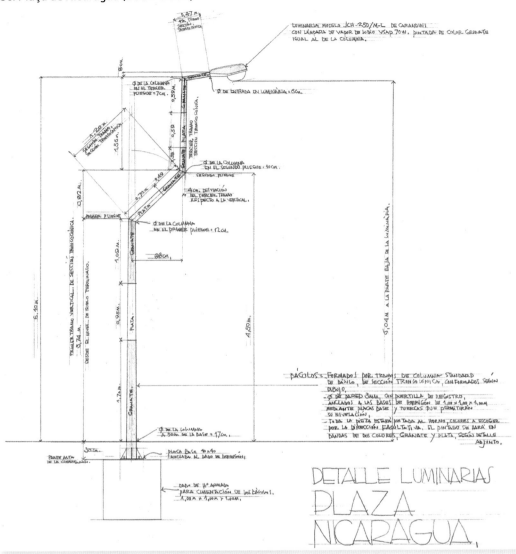

DETALLE LUMINARIAS
PLAZA
NICARAGUA

VEGETAL WALL
Retaining wall systems in three parks (2000-2007)

Location Parc de Ca n'Oriol, Rubí (A4a); Parque de la Vaguada de las Llamas, Santander (A4b); Vall d'en Joan, Carretera de la Sentiu, Gavà (A4c)
Client Ajuntament de Rubí (A4a); Ayuntamiento de Santander (A4b); Entitat Metropolitana de Residus, Diputació de Barcelona, Mancomunitat de Municipis de l'Àrea Metropolitana de Barcelona, Ministerio de Hacienda (A4c)
Authors Enric Batlle, Joan Roig | www.batlleiroig.com
Teresa Galí-Izard, paisajista (A4b, A4c)
Collaborators Elena Mostazo, paisajista (A4a, A4b), Xavi Ramoneda (A4a), Albert Gil (A4b), Jordi Nebot (A4c)
Construction and technology consultant Antonio Casado, Acycsa
Photographs Batlle i Roig, Eva Serrats (A4c)

Building in public spaces poses specific demands on the use of materials and components, especially when it is about a large-scale landscape intervention. Whereas the indiscriminate use of concrete or steel structures is unquestioned in architecture, whether in the whole project or for certain technical requirements, the presence of powerful structural elements in landscaping projects can interfere or contradict other specific design solutions. Landscaping implies going deep into the field of gardening, and thus taking on the language and tone of plants and minerals. The most demanding case is probably the design of slopes and retaining walls, since a certain contradiction exists between the tectonic character of these structures and the plant or mineral characteristics of a park. To resolve this contradiction, we tried to design slopes and walls that would bring us closer to the general character desired for a park.

To exemplify this line of work, we present three projects where the elements of vertical retention were resolved using mineral elements: the park of Ca n'Oriol in Rubí, the park of la Vaguada de Las Llamas in Santander, and the landscaping of the former landfill of El Garraf in Barcelona.

In the park of Ca n'Oriol (page 34), a natural slope was reconfigured to allow for a comfortable pedestrian path. In order to ensure the sufficient width for the path, a practically vertical retaining wall had to be built. This wall was treated with a system steel rods that reinforce the soil and a metal mesh defining the almost vertical surface, on which an invading plant species that would cover the entire structure in a short time was planted. The contrast between the bushes of the slope and the planting of the path wall reveals a clearly articificial cut, but consistent with the general park system.

In the project of La Vaguada de Las Llamas (page 36), the wall was to compensate the three different levels the park was on. Given its inevitable visibility, it was decided that the wall would acquire a representative value, almost until becoming the defining image of the place. This suggested presenting the wall in a formally attractive way even before vegetation grew on it, even if the Atlantic climate of Santander would guarantee a full plant coverage in a period of six months. We chose a construction system made of stone and wood slabs, held up in a metal sling, supported on the massive rock wall that defines the slope. The vegetation on these slabs was laid out in a variety of small terraces, which gave the slope a clearly artificial image, not only because of its steepness but also because of such an arbitrary placement.

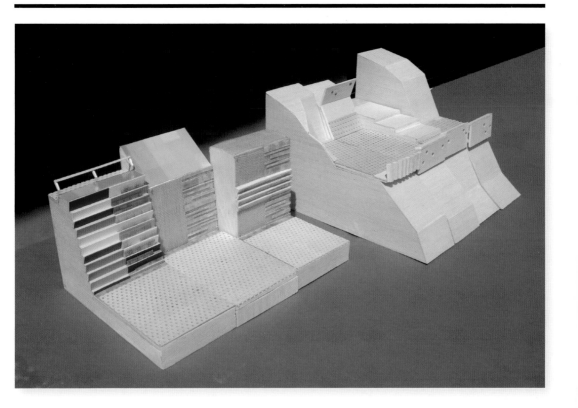

In the renovation of the former Garraf landfill (page 38), the gentle slopes that made up the topography did not require anything more than a coconut mesh covering to hold in place and protect the recently planted vegetation. However, the need to create a parking lot at the entrance of the grounds led us to devise a vertical wall system made of stone and earth that could also be invaded by occasional planting. The retaining structure of the wall is defined by a steel mesh filled with stone and which, In turn, supports a series of randomly placed earth trays that are planted with invading vegetation. These metal structures, given their shape and volume, could also be filled with any type of material. Some of them were used as a deposit for bales of trash, to demonstrate the industrial origins of the location.

These walls and slopes were designed and built with the help of Antonio Casado, owner of Acycsa, and in collaboration with Teresa Galí and Elena Mostazo.

A4a. Park of Ca n'Oriol

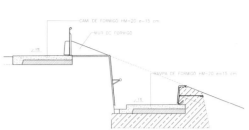

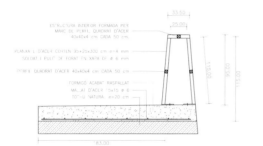

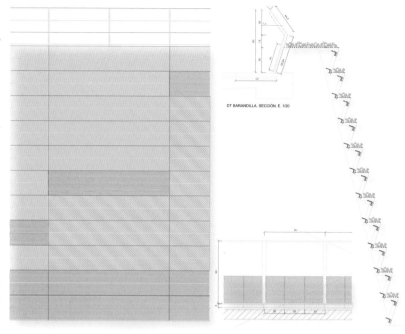

DT BARANDILLA. SECCIÓN. E. 1/20

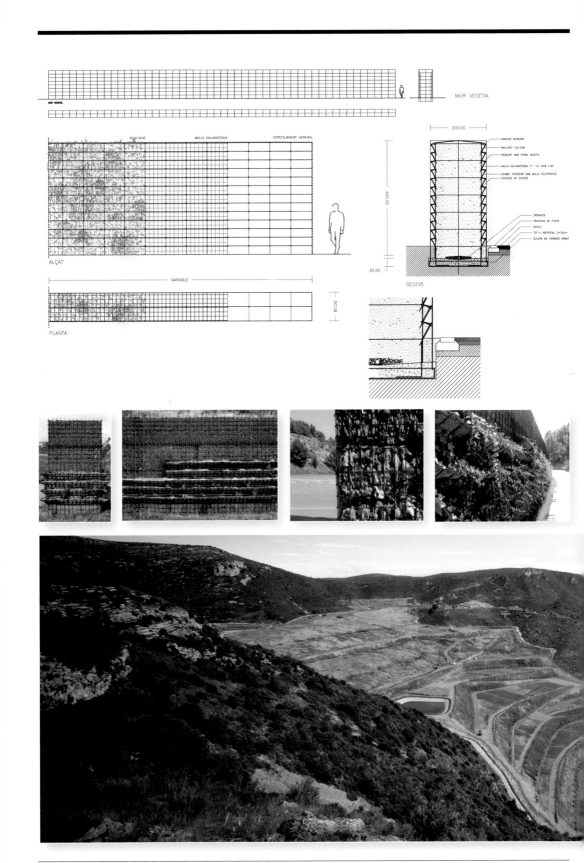

MUR VEGETAL

VEGETACIÓ   MALLA GALVANITZADA   ESPECEJAMENT GENERAL

ALÇAT

VARIABLE

PLANTA

200.00

CABLES TENSORS
MALLAZO 15x15x8
REBLERT AMB TERRA VEGETAL
MALLA GALVANITZADA T.T. 10-15x8 C.80
ACABAT EXTERIOR AMB MALLA POLIPROPILÈ
ESTESES DE GOTERS

DRENATGE
TRAVESSA DE FUSTA
ASFALT
TOT-U ARTIFICIAL G=20cm
SOLERA DE FORMIGÓ ARMAT

SECCIÓ

LIGHT BRIDGE
Pedestrian catwalk (2002-2003)

Location Parc de Vallparadís, Terrassa
Client Pla Director de les Esglésies de Sant Pere de Terrassa
Authors RGA Arquitectes and Enginyeria Reventós, S.L.
based on an original concept by Pere Riera, Franc Fernández and Manel Reventós (1995)
RGA Arquitectes: Pere Riera, Josep M. Gutiérrez, Josep Sotorres, Montserrat Batlle,
Barto Busom | www.rga.es
Engineering Portell-Brunés Enginyers, S.L.
Contractor ACSA Agbar Construcción, S.A.
Area 216 m²
Budget € 566.000
Photographs Lourdes Jansana, RGA

This footbridge, with a width of 2.7 m and a thickness of only 28 cm (L/286) has a span of 90 m. It responds to the structural scheme of a prestressed concrete ribbon bridge with a central deflection of 1.67 m (L/48) and a difference in height between the beggining points of the ribbon of 1.8 m.

The first human-built bridges to overcome wide spans were in the form of the catenary, the typology of the suspension bridge. Even today, the suspension bridge is the only existing technology for very long spans. Materials, however, have evolved: first lianas, then ropes, later on chains, and finally cables.

Contrary to bridges for vehicles, on pedestrian bridges one can unify the structural components and the walking platform in one single element. Luckily, human beings are less demanding than machines to be able to move comfortably. We also weigh much less than any vehicle. The structures that the support of the suspension bridge use and that unify cable and platform receive the name of stressed ribbon. Its main characteristic is that it does not need towers to suspend the cables from, since the geometry of the platform — the catenary arc — is what provides stiffness to the structure.

As in all cases of suspended structure, the critical element is the anchoring of the strong horizontal forces that are generated. As for the rest, the construction procedure is extraordinarily simple and the entire board can be prefabricated.

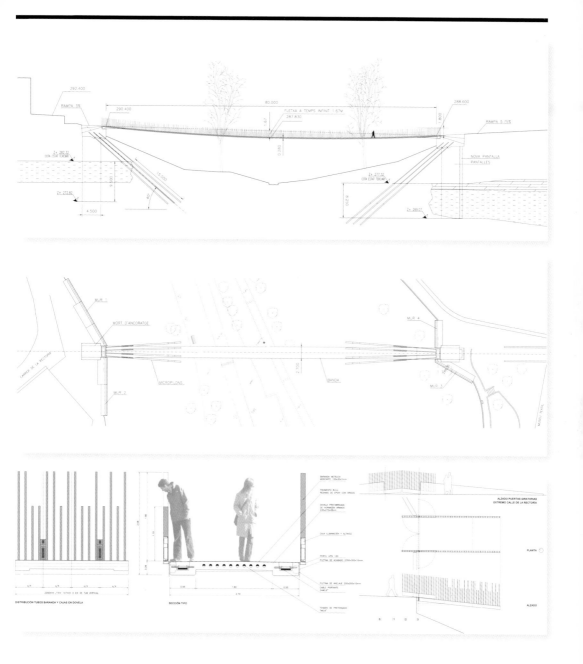

DISTRIBUCIÓN TUBOS BARANDA Y CAJAS EN DOVELA

SECCIÓN TIPO

STRUCTURAL GLASS
FF: Ferran Figuerola, Cricursa
JT: Joan Tarrús, Cricursa
JF: Jordi Fernández, ON-A
EG: Eduardo Gutiérrez, ON-A

JT The project for the Cricursa stand at the Construmat 2007 fair marks a new stage for the company. At previous editions of the fair we built stands which were intended principally to demonstrate the geometric complexity that we could achieve in glass production. But when we contacted On_a architects we also asked them to produce an architectural concept, not just a platform for displaying the product.

FF At first our stands were simply a base on which we placed a table, two chairs, glass samples... and that was it! Then we contracted the services of interior designers who created a more attractive space for displaying the samples, although the space itself was not identified with the company. Eventually we realized that, if our business specializes in the definition of architectural spaces, that was precisely what we had to create: an architectural space that spoke for the company and was attractive to the public.

JF Our first approach to this commission was to fit in a programme: a meeting room, an audiovisual projection space, the display of the product itself... Given that this stand had to be reassembled later at other fairs, we did an analysis of the lowest common denominator space in which it had to fit: a seven-by-ten-metre rectangle. Inside we defined four environments: a space for the presentation of the company, another for displaying the products, an area in which works done by Cricursa are presented, and, finally, a material display in the form of the stand itself of the application of the different types of glass: curved, spherical, large flat acid-treated pieces. The point of reference for the physical organisation of these environments was the structure of the material itself, the form in which silica is found in nature. The aim was to build a crystalline structure based on the conditioning factors of the glass and the programme. The three colours used correspond to the three types of glass with which the stand was built. The structure was also based on its itinerancy from one fair to the next. From the outset, we conceived of a prototype of the structural node, with its connections and bars, which would permit the adaptation of all the geometries of the faces of the pavilion.

FF The construction of the stand became, in fact, an example of the relations we establish with architects. We've been in the business a long time and this has given us the chance to develop very close relationships and conceive of, with those architects, new prototypes that adapt to the applications they want to achieve. It is an industrial activity which forms part of a very powerful creative process that is in turn closely linked to the development of new technological applications.

EG   This will to explore finds its match in many young architects' desire to innovate. We might say that there are two types of companies: those that are enthusiastic about their work and want to progress and learn constantly, and those that don't; those that release a product on to the market and sit back, and you can't convince that they should change their attitude. Of course, the most innovative architects want to work with the first type of company, which is willing to research, to develop new prototypes, try out new technologies, new effects, which identifies with a project of this type.

JT   In the early 1990s we brought a new product out on the market, transparent solar control glass, and we launched a campaign aimed at presenting it to architects with personal visits to their offices. And we all know how architects, at least good ones, when you show them a product, they immediately ask you to change it and develop applications for their projects. It is this dialogue, this two-way relationship, that produces innovation.

JF   The stand also ended up acting as a demonstration of the possibilities of the material. The architects that saw it inevitably thought about their own projects: if this is possible, why not try it and adapt it?

EG   Our project pushes the limits of the size and, above all, the curving of glass, but also its handling. In order to move large pieces of glass, curved in two directions and of a considerable weight you need special machinery and technologies.

JT   And we also had to push the limits on production and assembly time, reducing the margin for error, for defects in a material whose production includes laminating, acid treatment, curving and folding to attain the desired geometry...

FF   Before the fair we only did one trial assembly of the structure. So at the fair we had to get it right. This degree of difficulty and the fact that we got ourselves involved so directly in the assembly helped us to understand better the vision of the architect and the process of the construction of a building.

JF   This, indeed, teaches a great deal about how to have more effective communication with the architect. We can establish a dialogue, not only about the form of the glass, but also about its fitting. And thus develop faster, more feasible solutions.

STRUCTURAL GLASS
Fair stand (2006-2007)

Location Fira de Barcelona, Construmat 2007
Client CRICURSA
Architects Jordi Fernández, Eduardo Gutiérrez (ON-A) | www.on-a-lab.com
Design team Jordi Farell, Carlos García-Sancho (ON-A)
Graphic design Bernardo Magalhaes (ON-A)
Structural engineering Technical Department, CRICURSA
Sound and image projections GROTESK
Glass and steel structure CRICURSA
Acid engraving and vinyl GRABACID
Woodwork CALPEMA
Carpet SERINKJET
Photographs Lluís Ros

We started with the base material for glass making, silica, which is found in several minerals such as quartz, in crystalline formations where general polyhedric volumes thread among themselves, parting from a common base and generating gaps between them. We wanted an architecture that would connect humans to nature.

Its geometry, derived from the brief, is manipulated, carved and modeled as a jeweler would cut a diamond, giving value and weight to each of the different parts that make up the object. The definition of this constructive process meant constantly going from virtual to real. Each material has its specific characteristics, weight, resistance, and maximum production dimensions. From these premises, the definitive model arises, both in shape and in constructive system — a wire frame of folded steel plates screwed together, so as to create a stable mesh, capable of holding the weight of the crystalline sides. The glass panels are supported by the mesh and also provide stability to the structure, thus moving from ornamental simplicity to structural funcionality.

Three different types of glass were used, organized according to the company's colors: flat glass in orange-yellow, creased glass (two distinct planes united by a curve) in orange, and spherical glass in a blue color and of a convex surface, with a central deflection of up to 20 cm. Each glass had a different shape and engraved patterns that provided different degrees of transparency.

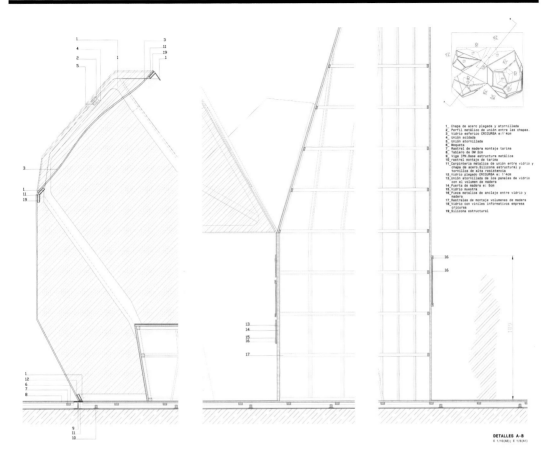

1_ Chapa de acero plegada y atornillada
2_ Perfil metálico de unión entre las chapas.
3_ Vidrio esférico CRICURSA e:1'4cm
4_ Unión soldada
5_ Unión atornillada
6_ Moqueta
7_ Rastrel de madera montaje tarima
8_ Tablero de DM 2cm
9_ Viga IPN.Base estructura metálica
10_ rastrel montaje de tarima
11_ Carpintería metálica de unión entre vidrio y
     chapa de acero.Silicona estructural y
     tornillos de alta resistencia
12_ Vidrio plegado CRICURSA e: 1'4cm
13_ Unión atornillada de los paneles de vidrio
     con el volumen de madera
14_ Puerta de madera e: 5cm
15_ Vidrio muestra
16_ Pieza metálica de anclaje entre vidrio y
     madera
17_ Rastreles de montaje volumenes de madera
18_ Vidrio con viniles informativos empresa
     cricursa
19_ Silicona estructural

DETALLES A-B
E 1/10(A3); E 1/5(A1)

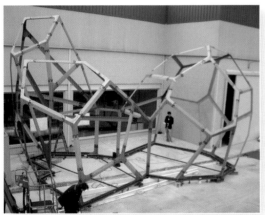

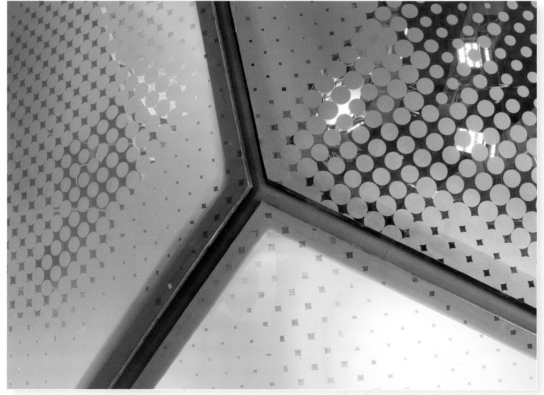

SKIN

LAYER FRAME I (IMPROVED BALLOON FRAME)
House 5.15 (2000-2002)

Location Lles de Cerdanya
Client Xavier Garriga, Conxita Poch
Architect Arturo Frediani
Collaborator Francesc Oller
Structure Static Engineering
Technical Architect Mercè Martín Valls
Contractor Construccions i Restauracions Peypoch
Woodwork Fusteria El Pí
Structure and metal frames Buscall
Plot area 361.39 m²
Total floor area 343.32 m²
Budget € 312,500
Photographs Ramon Prat

The concept of Layered Balloon Frame (LBF) originates in the project for House 5.15. The special characteristics of the façade required a precise fitting of the large wooden shutters, some of them measuring up to 7 m². In the traditional balloon frame, the different façade layers are supported on a wood frame structure. As the wood ages and reacts to humidity, these balloon-frame buildings become deformed, reducing the operability of the windows and shutters. The LBF divides up the responsibilities, separating structure from skin, loads and materials. The structure and framework are built in steel while the filling can be done in wood without compromising the dimensional stability of the whole. The tolerance of steel guarantees smooth movement of large mechanisms. The pendular shutters with sliding movement of House 5.15 benefit from the possibilities of a 'self-tech' system that allows half of the façade to effortlessly retract over the other half.

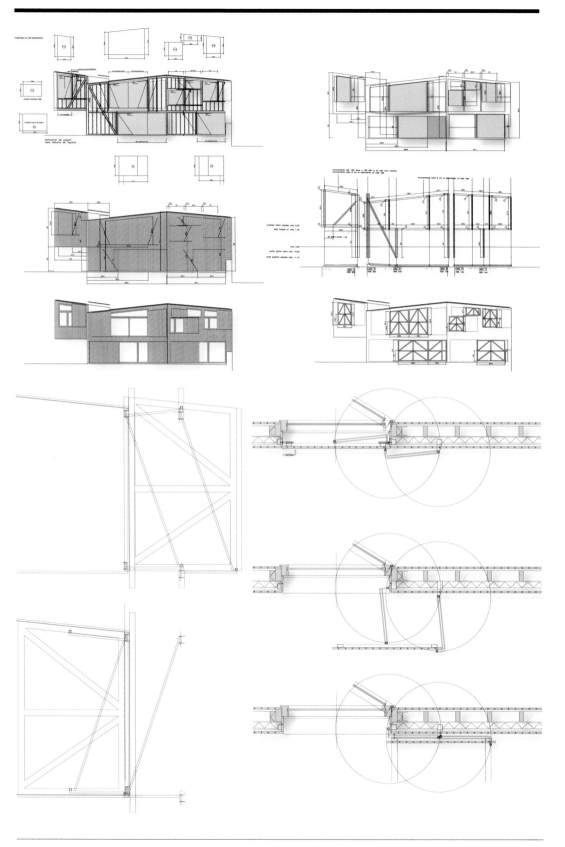

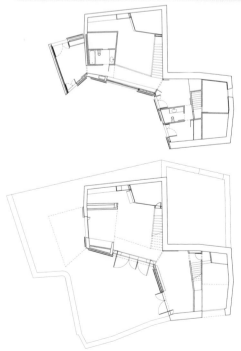

WRAPPED-LAYER FRAME II (TEXTILE FAÇADE OF EPDM)
12 social housing units (2004-2007)

Client Viserma Serveis i Manteniment, Ajuntament de Vilassar de Dalt
Architect Arturo Frediani
Designt team Jordi Colomer, Toni Valverde, Elisabet Prat
Technical architect Mercè Martín
Structure Gerardo Rodríguez, Static
EPDM Trelleborg
Contractor Excover
Total floor area 1,420 m²
Budget € 1,430,870
Photographs Arturo Frediani

These social housing units of 85 and 68 m² are designed in a way that the size of the living room (41 and 35 m² respectively) and its relationship with the façade have unconventional generosity. Entirely built with a steel structure and screwed panels, without with any concrete or mortar, the building is wrapped in an EPDM rubber façade reinforced with polyester fiber forming a cushion. Window frames slide along the front of the façade, turning the windows of the living rooms into balconies when they are opened.

The economy of the Layered Balloon Frame (LBF) system is based on extreme precision joined with a high execution speed and the possibility to correct occasional construction errors in a clean and almost instantaneous way. This experimental apartment building carried out for a small city near Barcelona reveals that strategies for public housing, especially those applied by the autonomous (regional) government, have been anchored in traditional construction systems that offer a low quality of finishes compared to what can be achieved for the same price.

Different specialized layers are placed (basically cut and screw) on the steel frame: insulating boards, drywall sheets, occasionally galvanized steel facing, and a continuous water-tight barrier formed by a sheet of polyester fiber-plaited EPDM rubber. The cushion effect of this material guarantees free movement of the building envelope. The material adheres by means of vulcanization thus forming a tailored continuous and impermeable suit for the building. Savings in construction costs are invested in the huge sliding, liftable windows.

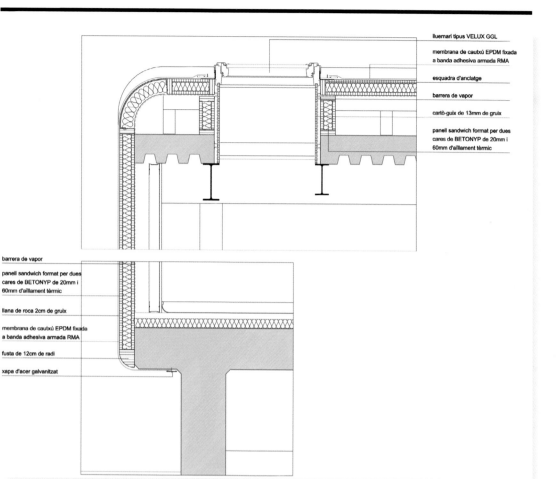

lluernari tipus VELUX GGL

membrana de cautxú EPDM fixada a banda adhesiva armada RMA

esquadra d'anclatge

barrera de vapor

cartó-guix de 13mm de gruix

panell sandwich format per dues cares de BETONYP de 20mm i 60mm d'aïllament tèrmic

barrera de vapor

panell sandwich format per dues cares de BETONYP de 20mm i 60mm d'aïllament tèrmic

llana de roca 2cm de gruix

membrana de cautxú EPDM fixada a banda adhesiva armada RMA

fusta de 12cm de radi

xapa d'acer galvanitzat

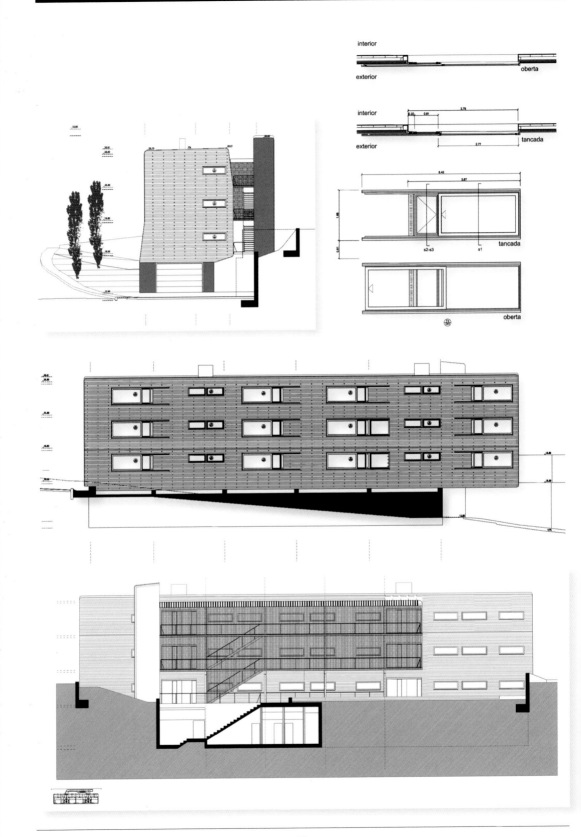

interior

oberta

exterior

interior

tancada

exterior

tancada

oberta

HIGHWAY FAÇADE
Car dealership (2003-2004)

Client Comercial Alari S.A.
Location Carrer Joan Costa i Deu, Sabadell
Architects EQUIP.XCL | www.xclaramunt.com
Xavier Claramunt, Martín Ezquerro, Miquel de Mas
Design team Yago Haro, Marc Zaballa, Josep Piera, Pau Vidal, Ho-Sang
Contractor Cycons
Technical Architect Joel Vives
Engineer Nadico, Jordi Codina
Metal frames Metal S.L., Efrén
Total floor area 6,280 m²
Budget € 3,568,000
Photography Adrià Goula

We are on a half-built plot partially occupied by three bays with a metal structure that must be turned into premises for a high-end car dealer. The original buildings are extended in two directions: the longitudinal extension of the three existing bays and the construction of half a bay on one of the sides, right up to the street edge. In the new wing, a metallic structure supports a roof that ascends as it approaches the street and ends up by crowning the façade with a curved line. This is the display space for the vehicles, where steel girders bridge the span between a line of pillars ant the continuous and self-supporting structure of the façade. The final manipulation of this space seeks the degree of comfort one might expect from a drawing room, a car sitting smoothly on a rug.

The aim is to shape a façade that will transform the building into an advertisement of itself. A metallic structure was erected to hold two shells. By means of fibre cement plates, the enclosure is built to make the building watertight and to finish the inside. The second one, more external and not waterthight, is made from mechanised stainless steel panels installed longitudinally, parallel to the streets and road. This curtain of waves shrinks at certain points to mark the accesses and to provide glimpses into the showroom. The scales of the glazed parts and of the curtain of waves imply two distances from which to perceive the building: one from the motorway and road, in movement, and another one a few meters from the building, static, from street level. The middle point is a no-man's-land. You are either far away, reading an advertising hoarding, or in front of the cars on display, about to walk into the building. The clue to interpreting the shape is provided by the protection barriers of the motorway, from where one has privileged views of the building. A fleeting brightness.

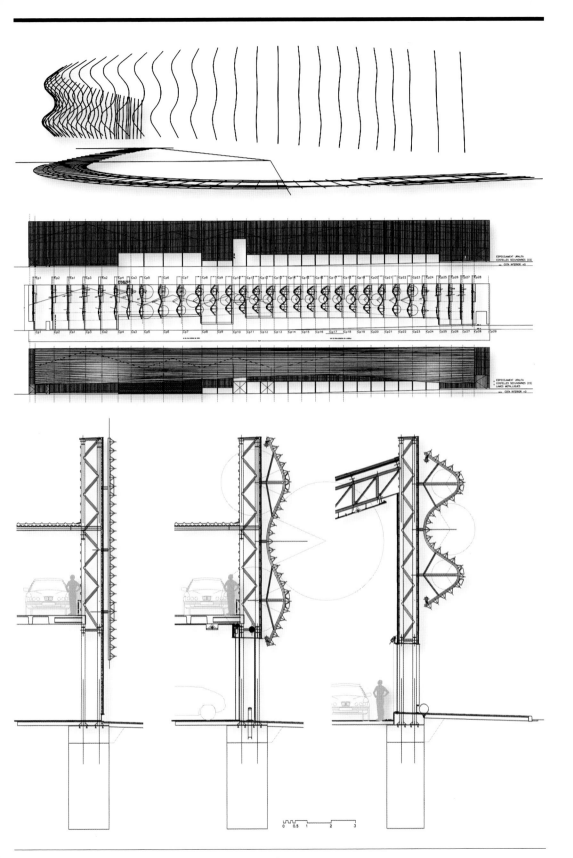

THE INTERACTION BETWEEN LOAD BEARING STRUCTURE AND FAÇADE
JLM: Josep Lluís Mateo, MAP Architects
AO: Agustí Obiol, BOMA

AO Pre-modern architects understood architecture as a sum of structure and decoration. The skin, according to this vision, is a defining component of the architecture. In Gothic, for example, the roof onfolds over the columns, the walls, the buttresses and flying buttresses. This has evolved and been mis-interpreted today in a specialization of the different elements of the building: the structure, the partitions, the enclosures, the fittings... All of them understood as design phases that are developed separately, independently. Now what we most need to recover from this classical vision is the value it assigned to the sum of the parts, the value of whole.

JLM I have always been interested in using structure as a fundamental, substantive, part of the project; and, at a primary level, as an ordering device that grounds the formal decisions, a first degree of structure in the sense of logical order, of Cartesian system. As the buildings we work on grow in size and the structures have to respond in a more evident manner to the forces of gravity, this argument becomes charged with energy. The first moment in which this approach came up in a clear form was in the design of the Barcelona International Convention Centre (CCIB), a building with steel columns and wide span beams, and in the two adjacent buildings: the CZF office block and the Hotel AC, which are tall towers with a small base, with concrete frames and walls. But it was in a competition for an office building in Zurich that I first valued as a work tool the stress diagrams produced by BOMA, of great visual value in themselves.

AO This project included some exceptional requirements on the part of the client, which meant we had to build very thick concrete walls with few openings in order to ensure a high level of thermal insulation. These basic conditions defined from the outset a possible structure for the building and enabled us to think about an interior free of columns.

JLM The relation imposed in the façade between solid and hollow, between wall and window, excluded the possibility of a structure encased in a more or less conventional curtain wall, as usually happens in these office buildings. Moreover, all the demands of the commission pointed to a building similar to its neighbours, a conventional urban construction, with load-bearing walls and a composition of windows in accordance. Our project began, in fact, as a response to the physical context, the requirements of the brief, and the local building codes. The structural diagrams that BOMA did based on the geometries generated by these first responses produced a highly defined expression of the form of the façade, with a fenestration that was a result of the structural requirements. Thus the structural plan became the plan of the façades. This is organic architecture in the most basic sense of the term, where all the decisions are the product of a single internal logic.

AO There is a point in the history of architecture where the skin ceases to be thought of as structure, when these two elements are segregated from each other. The new integration we are working with there-fore links us to certain logic from the past, but with materials that have structural capacities and features which are much superior to those attained two or three hundred years ago.

JLM And we also have increasingly sophisticated instruments of calculation, with formally very rich systems of visualization, which enable you to assess the thickness and geometry of each structural element in function of the project decisions, and intervene in them accordingly. We could say that all those studies that Gaudí did on the basis of physical models happen now almost immediately.

AO   The calculation programmes also enable you to visualize very quickly how the structure responds to modifications in the geometry, the loads and the materials, and thus the stresses represented. This process of visualization was used very directly in the design of the Sociópolis apartment building in Valencia. The key to this project is the laminate treatment of the façade: rather than as a framed element, understanding it as a continuous structural skin, which lends it enormous load-bearing capacity. This was, for example, the model of the façades of the Twin Towers in New York, which, though at first sight seemed to be built based on a steel skeleton, with columns and beams, the façade was in fact a very dense structural web of steel, with voids – windows – in just 45% of surface area, and 55% solid. Rather than a framed structure, it was perforated steel wall. The collapse of the structure did not occur due to the rupture of the façade, but to the implosion of the inner core. There is classical definition of structure which sees it as the relation between material and geometry, and in fact that is our approach. The same material used in different situations can become a column, a beam or an arch. Therefore, the geometry is what finally formalizes the structure, it is the point of departure set out by MAP Architects, and it will be redefined in accordance with the calculations. At this point in time, the calculation programmes themselves enable you to define the optimum form of the structure: you define the perimeter, a set of loads and a set of supporting points; the programme generates a framework of finite elements, analyzes it, sees which elements take no loads, eliminates them... and in this way it comes up with the structure. I have always said that most perfect structure is the human body, because it redefines itself, concentrating and reducing the bone mass to only those parts in which it bears loads and transmits them. The areas that are not involved in this load-transmission system end up disappearing. This is the process that these programmes reproduce.

MULTIPERFORATED SKIN
Barcelona International Convention Centre, CCIB
(2000-2004)

Client Ajuntament de Barcelona, Barcelona Regional, Infraestructures del Llevant
Location Recinte Fòrum, Barcelona
Architects MAP Architects | www.mateo-maparchitect.com
Josep Lluís Mateo, Marta Cervelló, Jordi Pagès
Design team Anna Llimona, Marc Camallonga, David Carim, Virginia Daroca, Lucas Eche-veste, Pasqual Bendicho, Yolanda Olmo, Carlos Montalbán, Héctor Mendoza, Xavier Monclús, Elsa Bertran, Pilar Ferreres, Luis Falcón, Odon Esteban, Cristina Pardal, Nacho López, Alexis López, Eva Egler
Structural design Obiol, Moya y Asociados, Agustí Obiol | www.bomasl.net
Consulting engineer at preliminary design stage Werner Sobek Ingenieure
Façade consultants Biosca + Botey S.A.: Xavier Ferrés with José Fernández Blasco, Eber Rueda, Javier García, Marta Cases
M&E engineering OIT / INDUS
Lightng ARUP-Spain
Acoustics Estudi Acústic Higini Arau
Project management IDOM
Contractors FCC, Ferrovial, COMSA
Photographs Ramon Prat, Oriol Rigat, Fòrum Barcelona 2004/Albert Masias, MAP

The Barcelona International Convention Centre (CCIB) is made up of a large dividable hall (15,000 m², 80 m structural span) and an adjoining services block that is open to the sea. The hall is structure and abstraction; the outer block speaks to the sea and sky. The structure is the score. The climate, light (and its opposite, shade), sound (and its opposite, silence) are its themes: the flows of people and of not-so-diverse fluids, the masses and the architecture that appears and frequently disappears among them.

The southern and western wings were to relate to the garden immediately next to it as well as with the sky and the nearby sea, something that suggested using organic mechanisms in the definition of structure and form — geometries that were not strictly Cartesian. Relating the theme to the structural logic of the building enclosure, we define a façade made of aluminium panels supported on the horizontal floor slabs, a sort of curtain whose small pleats configured a warped surface defined by a series of relatively flat generatrixes.

The panel's surface could be manipulated in two ways, by perforating it with variable dimensions or by embossing it, making incisions in it without actually perforating it, also with wide margins of freedom. This double possibility of finishing (perforated or embossed), allows us to define a continuous skin regardless of the degree of transparency required for functional reasons. Although each piece is different, the logic of the general construction is the same.

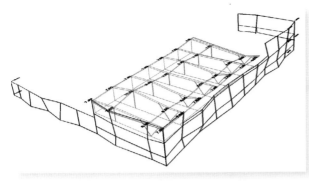

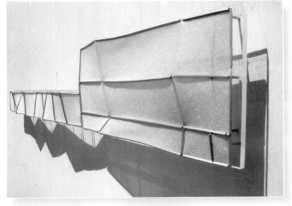

diagonales martelé plata

pörtico
oxirón negro

tubo perimetral+ anclajes galvan.
martelé plata

anclajes
oxirón negro

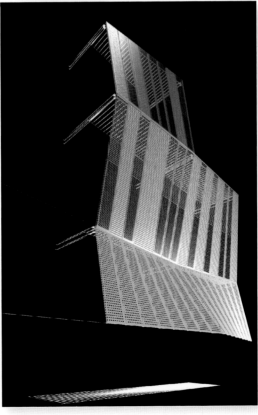

PERFORACIÓN: densidad P1>P3
REPUJADO: densidad R1>R3

● PANELES CON FIJACCION ESPECIAL PARA ACCESO DE BOMBEROS

0   10   50   100

PERFORACIÓN: densidad P1>P3
REPUJADO: densidad R1>R3

0   10   50   100

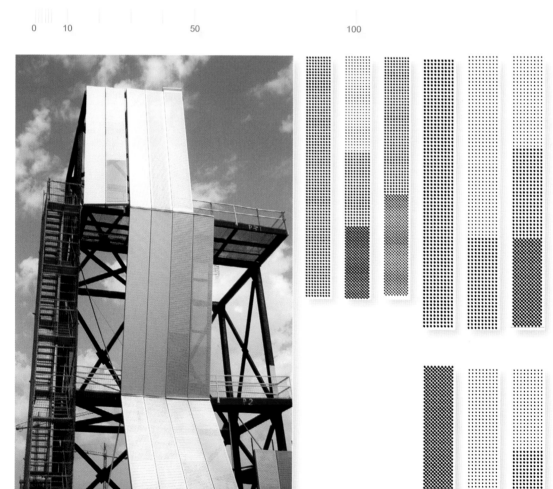

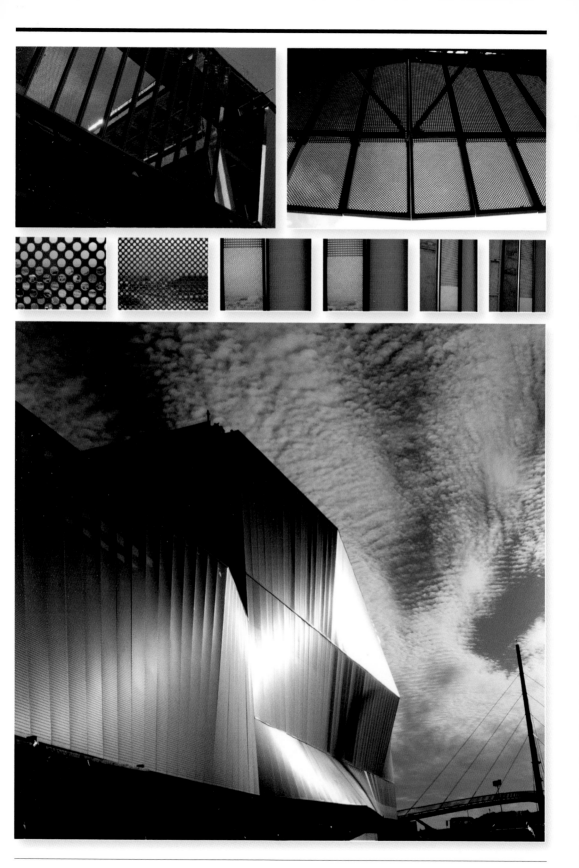

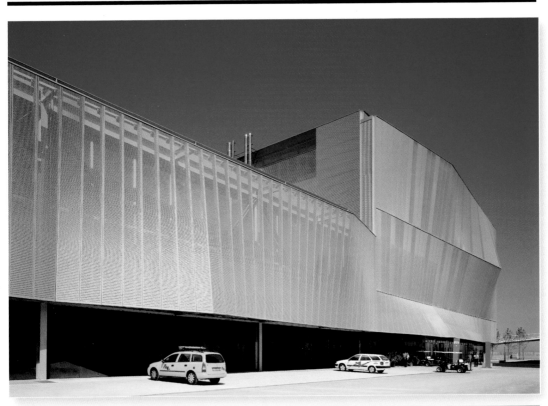

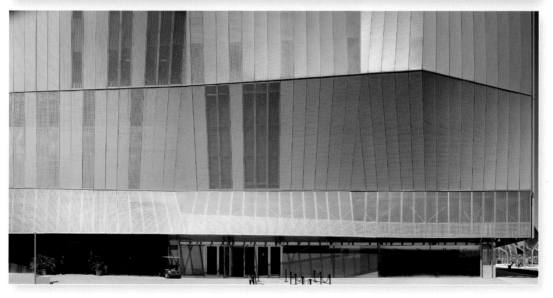

JALOUSIE WALL
Day center for elderly people (2005-2007)

Client Ajuntament de Cardedeu
Location Carrer Llinars, Cardedeu
Architects F451 Arquitectura | www.f451arquitectura.com
Toni Montes, Santi Ibarra, Lluís Ortega, Xavier Osarte, Esther Segura
Technical architect Teresa Vivó
Structural engineering J. M. Riba de Palau
Geotechnical studies TEC-SOL
Landscape architect Teresa Galí-Izard
Contractor Abelcir, S.L.
Ceramic façade Blau, S.L.
Budget € 612,000

The urban context provided quite a bit of information to define the proposal. On one hand, the area is in the middle of a process of transformation, with the foreseen construction of a series of low-rise apartment buildings that will take up three corners of the block. Our building is located on the part of the block that is assigned to municipal facilities, surrounded by an old textile factory of great architectural quality, characterized by the uniformness established by the sequence of bays and the chromatic homogeneity of its ceramic structural and façade components. Our design approach originated from these two considerations, along with the wish to provide the center with multiple relationships between inside and outside spaces and at the same time preserve a certain privacy.

The relationship with the context is defined by two decisions:
1. The building is organized in three structural bays, similar in orientation and spans to those of the adjacent factory buildings. By means of alternating empty spaces, a series of patios that relate to inside spaces are defined. The last of these patios corresponds to entrance area at the corner of the block, open to the streets.
2. The integration of the day center with the textile factory is guaranteed by the facework material. All of the vertical skin of the building is done in ceramic materials. The blank walls, the latticework, and the louvers are done in different ceramic pieces, turning the façades into a monochromatic mosaic of changing textures.

Each space of the center, except the laundry area, has a direct relationship with the outdoors through different patios. The patios are specialized and their proportions and the pavement treatments respond to their function. Energetic, programmatic, and constructive sustainability are determining factors in all design decisions.

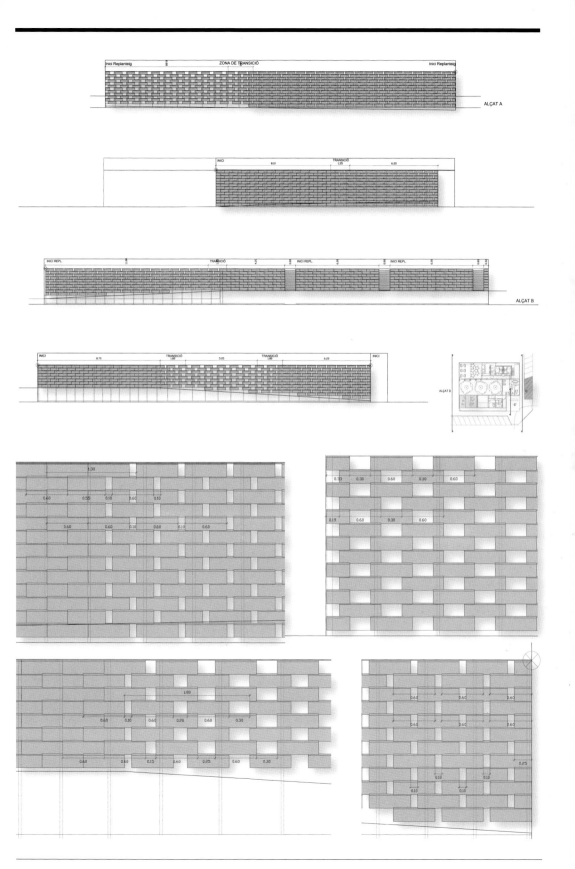

Inici Replanteig   ZONA DE TRANSICIÓ   Inici Replanteig

ALÇAT A

INICI   8.10   TRANSICIÓ   1.35   6.20

INICI REPL.   TRANSICIÓ   INICI REPL.   INICI REPL.

ALÇAT B

INICI   8.70   TRANSICIÓ   1.90   3.05   TRANSICIÓ   1.90   6.20   INICI

ALÇAT D

VISTA AERA DE LA COBERTA ECOLÒGICA

REVESTIMENT EXTERIOR

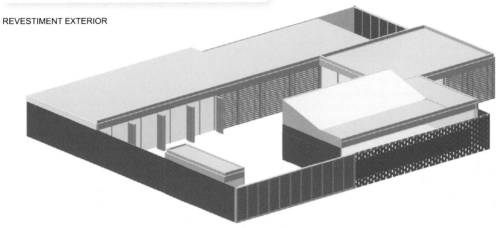

REVESTIMENT INTERIOR

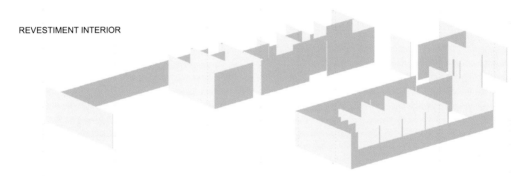

ESTRUCTURA

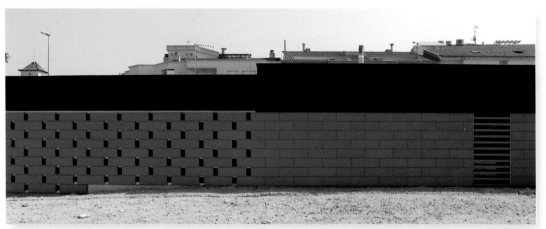

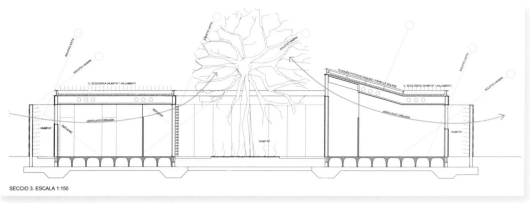

SECCIO 3. ESCALA 1:150

FILTER WALL
New Headquarters of the company
Eurocomercial de Nuevas Tecnologías, SL (2004-2006)

Developer EUROCONT - Eurcomercial de Nuevas Tecnologías, SL
Architects HYBRIDa: Sylvia Felipe, Jordi Truco
Design team Emmanuel Rufo Calderón González, Udo Thoennissen, Francesca Calvino, Marco Verde (HYBRIDa)
Façade engineering Technocladd-Coperfil, Ferran Sen
Structural consultant Estudi Punt 6, Antoni Casas
M&E Engineering Alfa Instal·lacions SA
Digital production TAD (Taller d'Arquitectura Digital), ESARQ-UIC
Management on site HYBRIDWORKS
Floor area 989 m²
Budget € 712,390
Photographs Iñigo Bujedo

The client needed to adapt an open-plan warehouse organized on two levels and turn it into a multipurpose space housing offices, technical assistance service, a spare parts storage space and a repair workshop. The company also looked for a strong image in line with its activity — new technologies for the building industry.

The essential part of the project was the definition of the inner façade of the building, an enveloping system that would integrate structural and environmental features, and would allow the organization of the different work areas. In this case, it was necessary to think about the partitioning system not as a threshold to divide inside and outside, but as a filter that would act as a mediator between different conditions of light, climate, and sound, as well as providing different degrees of visual permeability between work areas.

As a starting point, we researched the enveloping and structural characteristics of an egg shell, as seen under a microscope. Throughout the course of this exploration, we understood the structure as a high performance skin and the skin as a differential structure. This idea of efficiency fascinated us but the example only allowed us to extract some geometric principles for the design of an apparently chaotic fabric. To establish our pattern, we described some parametric variables and rules of growth. There is no subjective formal decision in the final design or composition. Work with CAD/CAM tools allowed the creation and production of this pattern, with a formalization derived from the logic of variation and mutation.

In the development of the project we worked closely with the engineering department of TECHNOCLADD to modify the standard light-partition system DynamicWall and turn it into a hybrid system with two layers of operable insulating glass and a third fixed layer of semitransparent acrylic glass with different porosities. This last layer is the one that produces different effects of light, climate, sound, and visual permeability.

Reglas para crear el patrón

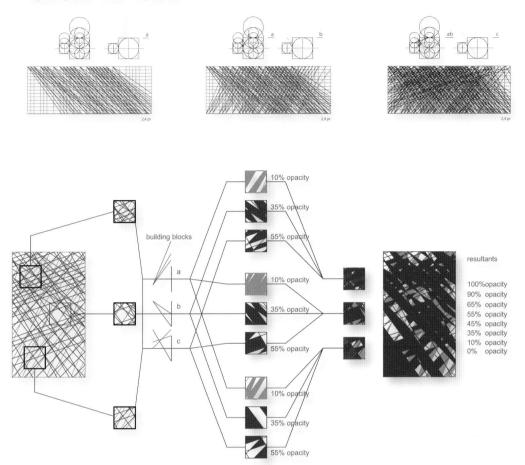

Reglas de opacidad_PATRON K-03

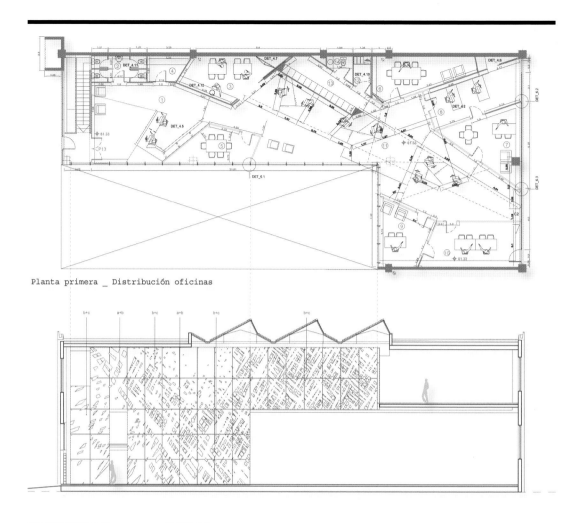

Planta primera _ Distribución oficinas

NURBS STRUCTURE
Villa Nurbs (2004-2008)

Location Empuriabrava, Castelló d'Empúries
Architect Enric Ruiz-Geli, Cloud 9 | www.e-cloud9.com | www.ruiz-geli.com
Project architect Felix Fassbinder, Jordi Fernández Río
Technical Architect Daniel Benito Pò, Xavier Badia, Agustí Mallol
Cloud 9 Team Miguel Carreiro, Emmanuel Ruffo, Rosa Duque, André Macedo, Ura Carvalho, Hye Young Yu, Marta Yebra, Mae Durant, Angelina Pinto, Randall Holl, William Arbizu, Max Zinnecker, Laia Jutgla, Manel Soler, Megan Kelly-Sweeney, Alessandra Faticanti, Susanne Bodach, André Brosel
Structural engineering BOMA SL
Contractor Obres i Construccions Joan Fustè
Piling Carsa
Metal structure Calderería Delgado
Metal frame and hydraulic works Ramon Presta
Installation Aiterm
Wood works Diorama
Inner skin Medio Design
M&E engineering PGI Group
Environmental advisor Estudi Ramon Folch
Design Emiliana Designestudio
Kitchen Artificio
Audiovisuals BAF
M&E equipment room Aislater, The Inox in Color
Landscape architect Jerónimo Hagerman
Photographs Luis Ros, Ramon Prat

Empuriabrava is an estate where the home is a morphing of the automobile space and boat space.

Process:
1. Experiment with the accident of the breaking of ice and obtain volumes of water.
2. Try to define a landscape, a landscape of pavilions, with the use of a natural material.
3. The construction of that landscape as a platform for living.
4. Measure and construct that landscape as a topography in 3D.
5. Its goal and reference will be a NURBS (Non-Uniform Rational B Spline).
6. Optimize constructive resources using CAD/CAM construction processes.
7. The architect creates that platform in a scalar progression: climate, geography, landscape, up to the skin of the home, the NURBS.
8. Invited industrial designers work from the skin of the NURBS all the way to the skin of the inhabitants, searching for a cellular and chemical approximation to materiality.
9. Definition of atmospheres inside the skin.
10. A skin with content. The skin has the capacity to absorb the hardware of the house.
11. The skin is reactive and manages energy and privacy, routes and movement of people, exposure to the wind and sun in different seasons. It is not an abstract design but the superimposition of different diagrams.

CERAMIC SKIN
Villa Nurbs

See general credits for Villa Nurbs in B7 (page 88)
Ceramic Ceràmica Cumella, S. L., Frederic Amat
Cables and fixtures Industrias BEC S.A.
Impermeability EPDM Roura i Pujol S. L.

The ceramic skin opens a new perspective in the field of architecture for the desfinition of façades. It is made up of a series of ceramic units designed in a way that, seen as a group, will work as if they were a wall of greenery. Depending on the direction they face, this skin has the capacity to protect the building from aggressive environmental conditions and from the sun, the rain, or strong winds, or otherwise to allow the sea breeze to permeate the structure.

A network of tensed cables fixed to the metal structure of the building hold these ceramic pieces up. Together they form the outer layer of the façade. By applying enamel, the painter Frederic Amat acts on each one of the ceramic pieces.

The geometry of these pieces is developed on a three-dimensional virtual model which is later produced following a digital fabrication process. These processes link computer-aided design software and CAM machine software that allows for the milling of wood pieces. The dialog between design software manufacturing software makes the physical production of the virtual model possible. Ceramics vs. the digital era.

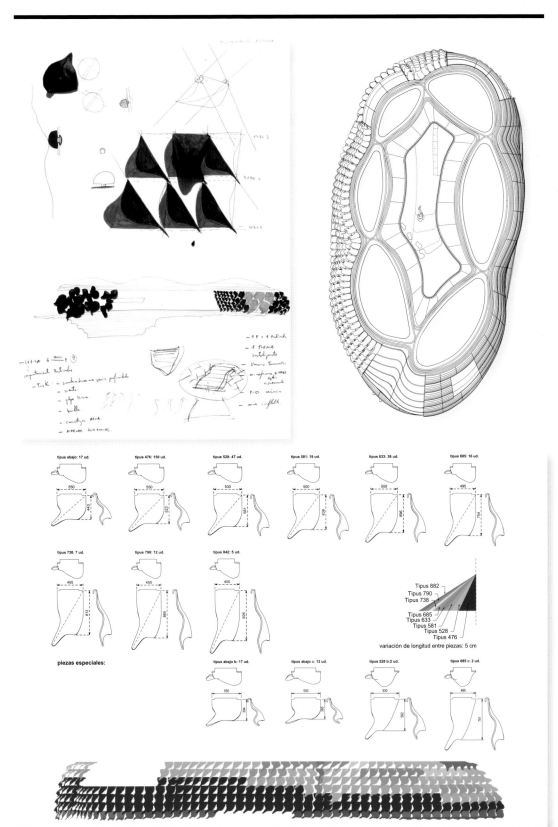

tipus abajo: 17 ud.

tipus 476: 150 ud.

tipus 528: 47 ud.

tipus 581: 19 ud.

tipus 633: 36 ud.

tipus 685: 16 ud.

tipus 738: 7 ud.

tipus 790: 12 ud.

tipus 842: 5 ud.

Tipus 882
Tipus 790
Tipus 738
Tipus 685
Tipus 633
Tipus 581
Tipus 528
Tipus 476

variación de longitud entre piezas: 5 cm

piezas especiales:

tipus abajo b: 17 ud.

tipus abajo c: 12 ud.

tipus 528 b:2 ud.

tipus 685 c: 2 ud.

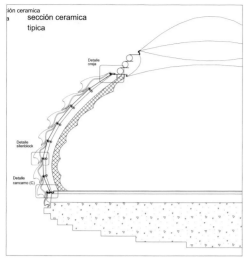

sección ceramica
sección ceramica
tipica

Detalle
oreja

Detalle
silenblock

Detalle
cancamo (C)

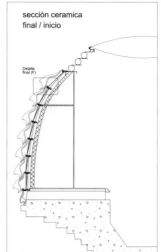

sección ceramica
final / inicio

Detalle
final (F)

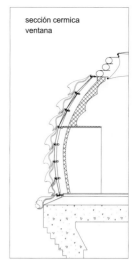

sección cermica
ventana

CORIAN SKIN
Villa Nurbs

See general credits for Villa Nurbs in B7 (page 88)
Corian skin Indústries de la Fusta Vilà
Glass Vicky Colombet, Dominique Chanin - Haim chanin fine Arts, Cricursa
Windows Jordi Roure

This is a skin-like façade system made up of deformed pieces of Corian, fixed to a network of tensed cables that is attached to the structure of the façade.

The specific shape of these pieces is acquired through a heating process, which gives them a characteristic elasticity, and enables their later placement on a mold.

Given that the materials that make up this façade are translucent (and transparent), the façade is also a translucent element.

The inner space can be flooded with outside daylight, and the light that comes from the inside can spread over the outer appearance at night. As long as there is a source of light, this is a façade that illuminates both inwardly and outwardly.

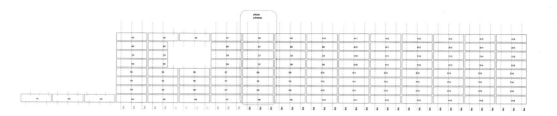

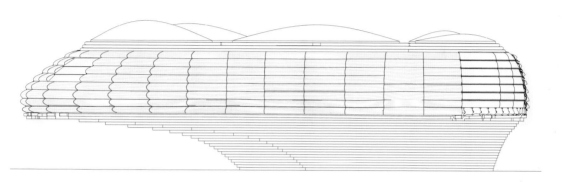

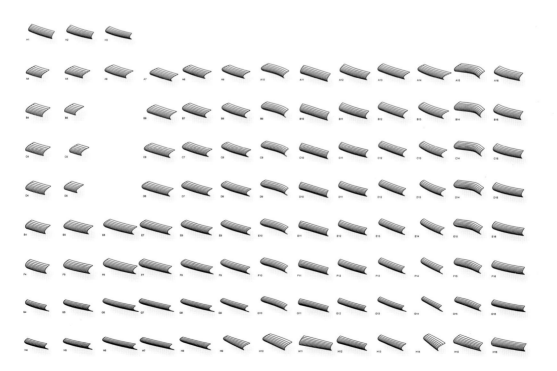

sección corian gota 01

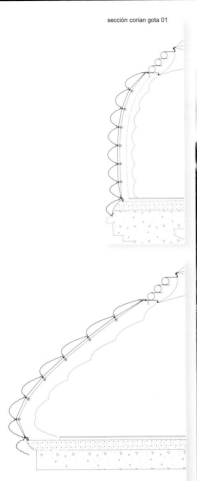

ETFE COVERING
Villa Nurbs

See general credits for Villa Nurbs in B7 (page 88)
ETFE Inflatables Covertex
FKM skin Tack Velas
Spa Pool Reindesa, Quimiprés
Covers Art Narac
Lighting Iguzzini, Leds Go

This is a new light roofing system made up of four layers of ETFE. Three of the layers are transparent (top and middle layers) and one is translucent (the inner, bottom layer). A supplementary sheet of 98% opaqueness with a circular pattern is divided between the two middle layers, which it adheres to. These layers define three inflatable elements or cushions that work with differential air pressures.

This is an almost immaterial covering. The sum of its five component layers make up a thickness of only 1.25 mm and 99% of its volume is air.

The pneumatic daylight control system is regulated by the air pressure in the inflatable upper and inner cavities, which allows the layer of ETFE that separates these two cushions to go up or down, and the two parts of the opaque sheet set among the inner layers to come in contact with each other.

The fact that there are several cushions and thus several air spaces makes it also a good thermal and acoustic insulation system.

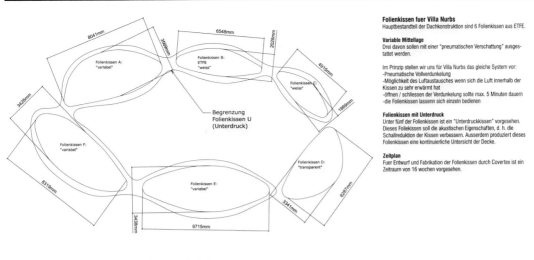

Folienkissen fuer Villa Nurbs
Hauptbestandteil der Dachkonstruktion sind 6 Folienkissen aus ETFE.

Variable Mittellage
Drei davon sollen mit einer "pneumatischen Verschattung" ausgestattet werden.

Im Prinzip stellen wir uns für Villa Nurbs das gleiche System vor:
-Pneumatische Vollverdunkelung
-Möglichkeit des Luftaustausches wenn sich die Luft innerhalb der Kissen zu sehr erwärmt hat
-öffnen / schliessen der Verdunkelung sollte max. 5 Minuten dauern
-die Folienkissen lassenn sich einzeln bedienen

Folienkissen mit Unterdruck
Unter fünf der Folienkissen ist ein "Unterdruckkissen" vorgesehen. Dieses Folienkissen soll die akustischen Eigenschaften, d. h. die Schallreduktion der Kissen verbessern. Ausserdem produziert dieses Folienkissen eine kontinuierliche Untersicht der Decke.

Zeitplan
Fuer Entwurf und Fabrikation der Folienkissen durch Covertex ist ein Zeitraum von 16 wochen vorgesehen.

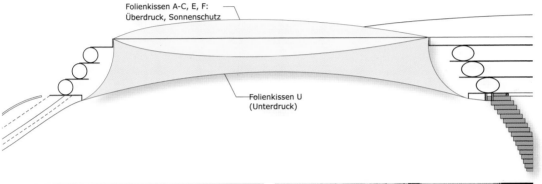

Folienkissen A-C, E, F: Überdruck, Sonnenschutz

Folienkissen U (Unterdruck)

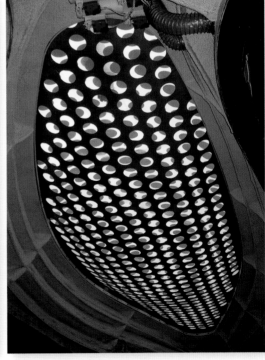

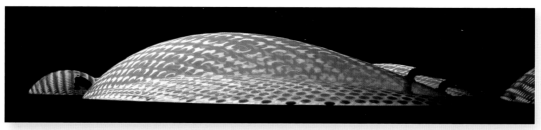

THE PERFECTIBLE FAÇADE: THE MECHANISMS OF ADAPTATION TO CHANGE
Ignacio Paricio

It is a cliché but that does not mean it is not true: change is the essence of our century and to assimilate it is the fundamental requirement of our culture. In the field of architecture, this is a requirement that the lightweight façade can meet with extraordinary effectiveness.

Perfectibility is the quality of being susceptible to improvement. In the production of goods, the concept of "perfectiblity" refers to the industry's capacity to offer initially simple products that can later be added on to and made more sophisticated in keeping with the user's demands, and financial resources. If a product is not perfectible, as our demands upon it grow, we eventually have no choice but to throw it out and buy a better one. The traditional analogic camera is an example of perfectibility; the digital version is not: any upgrade, the addition of megapixels, means buying a new machine, not the simple replacement of a microchip.

Buildings have a very long life in relation to the speed of change in society. A good architectural design must consider the possibility of change and adaptation in use over its lifespan. The incorporation of the concept of perfectibility in the skin of buildings refers in the first place to the openings, the perforations in the façade, in which a complex relation is established between the interior and exterior environments. Not only must the basic requirements of weathertightness and thermal comfort be resolved, but of similar importance are the control of solar radiation, ventilation and views. The more complex the requirements, the greater the range of accessories to incorporate. The window may be very simple in the first instance, but in order to meet future demands, it must be designed for all foreseeable upgrades, which should be easy and relatively inexpensive to perform, either by trained technicians or by the user himself.

Perfectibility of a window can be achieved with a subframe[1], to which one or more additional frames or other protective accessories can be subsequently fixed. Our approach with Technal to the perfectible window for the Casa Barcelona project at the 2001 Construmat fair was based on a basic deep subframe which could be upgraded with the addition of clip-on pieces, opening up an entire world of possibilities. First of all, a second frame, creating an air chamber to provide insulation against noise or extreme weather. It is easy to eventually fit very inexpensive solar protection inside this air chamber, as it would not be exposed to wind. The two frames with a sun screen inside can also make an excellent solar panel in winter. The space between the frames could also house an air-conditioning unit, given that the subframe can incorporate an electrical outlet and a moisture drainage system. Screens, plant pots for solar protection and many other types of fittings could be added to this perfectible window.

The perfectibility concept can be extended to the façade as a whole, which would mean complete industrialization and a vast range of possible changes, including replacing solid with void, and vice versa. It might seem that this latter sort of flexibility could be based on floor-to-floor façade panels, in other words, a system of compatible components. But the innumerable attempts made at introducing compatible components since the 1970s have all ended up in failure: the difficulties of adapting to the location or storing extremely expensive materials so far have frustrated a logical dream. The way to go seems to be the use of semiproducts — vertical and horizontal profile sections which form a framework suspended from the edges of the floor slabs into which solid panels or fixed and operable windows can be fitted.

---

1   Architectural aluminium, wholly pre-fabricated, cannot be subsequently re-sized to fit apertures cut into brickwork. Thus the rise of the subframe, a galvanized tubular element made on-site for precise fitting of the aluminium framing. It is essential that the subframe be fitted before finishing the brickwork, or even before the latter begins, if possible, in order to achieve perfect fitting and sealing of the joint between the subframe and the brickwork.

Technal offers a modular architectural aluminium system made up of 18cm-wide subframes, fixed to the edges of the floor slab, designed to hold a broad range of elements. One or two equal subframes can be attached to the inner or outer side of the original subframe, for total thicknesses of 36 or 54cm. Each subframe can hold either opaque or glazed panes, which later can be changed. The possible enclosures range from single-layer fixed or moveable panels to double-glazing with all sorts of elements within: shades, bars, moveable shutters or air-conditioning units.

Further components, including subframes and other elements, can be easily added to the original installation to adapt to each individual façade. The perfectible façade can be upgraded to meet new demands such as collecting solar energy or greater acoustic insulation. The approach is to start with a robust support in order to accommodate a diversity of add-ons, some of which have yet to be invented. But we must foresee the advent of continuous membranes, electronic control and intelligent materials.

Everything would seem to indicate that these innovations are only the start of a revolution in façade design in the 21st century. Where this will lead is hard to say. But it is likely that the façade will come to be seen as a membrane enclosure for the inhabited space, and that this will lead to the introduction of specific filters for the different flows passing through it: filters that are probably less physical and more chemical than those we have today; filters that can be activated electronically, like the electrochromic glazing and liquid crystal panels now used to give buildings instantly changing appearances.

PERFECTIBLE FAÇADE
"Illa de la Llum" residential towers (2001-2005)

Location Diagonal Mar (Sant Martí), Barcelona
Client Espais & Landscape Diagonal Mar, S.L.
Architects Lluís Clotet, Ignacio Paricio
Project leader Jordi Julián Gené
Project manager Javier Baqueró Rodríguez
Structural engineering NB-35 (Jesús Jiménez)
M&E engineering O.I.T. (Josep V. Martí Estelles i Miquel Camps)
Design team Ricardo Vázquez, M. Elena Plà, Victoria de León
Painter Anna Miquel
Landscape architect Bet Figueras
Budget € 20,631,685
Photographs Lluís Casals

The project proposes a 230-flat complex grouped, according to the masterplan, in three buildings: a 26-storey tower with a square section measuring a maximum of 28.5m per side; another 18-storey tower with a square section measuring a maximum of 24.5m per side; a long 5-storey building. The towers are designed for the maximum site occupation with the aim of favouring the arrangement of flats of different sizes and distributions. The excess of built area (limited to 32,940m^2) that would result from having all the floors equal in size is compensated by means of hollows in the volume which grow larger the higher we go. These voids are in the north-facing sides lacking sea views and in the areas closest to the other buildings.

Inside the towers, around each stairway and lift core, the floors are arranged in a series of bands. Immediately surrounding the core is the hallway which provides access to the flats. The next band, 50cm thick, is occupied by columns and mechanical and electrical pipes and fittings. The flats are organized troughout the widest band, 8m across, without any vertical structural element for maximum freedom of distribution. Another 50cm is also occupied by fittings, structure and the enclosures which separate the band of living space from the continuous terraces projecting 3 metres out. Due to their size and the protection from the sun and wind provided by sliding aluminium shutters, the terraces become a fundamental part of the dwelling, a connecting element between all rooms.

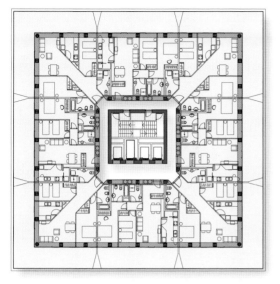

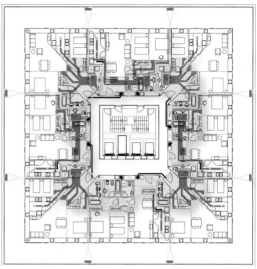

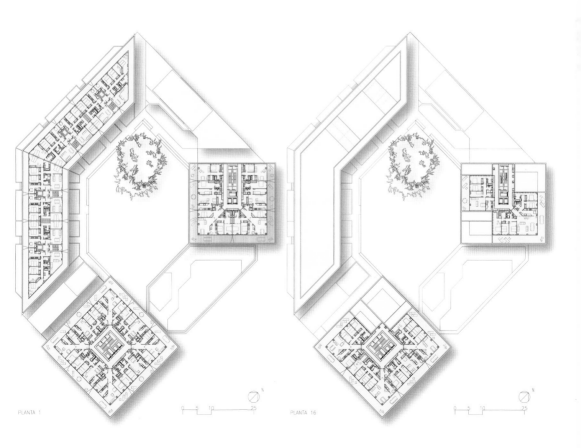

PLANTA 1

PLANTA 16

0 5 10   25

0 5 10   25

MEDITERRANEAN CURTAIN WALL

JC: Joan Comí, Sales Director, GET S.L.
RR: Ramon Ros, Director for East Zone, URSA
JS: Josep Solé, Technical Director, URSA
FP: Felipe Pich-Aguilera, Pich-Aguilera Arquitectes
TB: Teresa Batlle, Pich-Aguilera Arquitectes

FP   It all began with a commission for the refurbishment of an office building. This sort of building is usually associated with a transparent volume, enclosed in a curtain wall. But this sort of façade, which acts like a greenhouse, is hard to adapt to our climate. So we proposed adapting this system to Mediterranean conditions by making it selective in terms of daylight penetration, acting as an ultraviolet filter. We had already settled on the use of a lightweight material like polycarbonate instead of glass, which is much costlier and heavier and which would have required an aluminium framework in order to fix it in place.

JC   It was a time when the idea of sustainability was beginning to take hold in the building sector, which made us all aware of environmental problems, the need to use of recyclable products and energy savings. One requirement was a façade that would let light in, and evidently this meant designing in a solar control system.

FP   Your initial proposal to use a multilayer polycarbonate like Lexan Thermoclick had the advantage of low weight and simple fitting, which assured a huge savings in the glazing framework, but did not offer the level of thermal and acoustic insulation we wanted. With a simple double layer of the material, and ventilated chamber in between, this problem was solved. At first we though that this chamber could act as a heat source in winter, to keep the interior spaces comfortable, and so we would have to design an automatic or manual control system for the ventilation. But the tests we did showed that, even on the coldest winter days, the façade required a constant draw-off of heat, which greatly simplified the system. But that still left the problem of light control.

JC   The product in itself works to a certain extent as a screen, but it still let in too much light, and thus produced heat. In the façade system you proposed, with a natural hot air convection, the way to obtain the desired deflection of sunlight was in a treatment of the surface of the material: in this case, dot-printing with reflective ink. It is important to distinguish between ultraviolet and near infrared rays, which is what usually creates additional heat. The polycarbonate panel already has an ultraviolet filter on its outer face, because it is a material which is sensitive to radiation and without this protection it would yellow. The treatment of the inner face with this printing process would enable us to add the infrared filter and thus avoid heat accumulation without blocking out the sunlight.

FP   It was then that it occurred to us to give it an overall colour treatment, to infuse the interior with coloured light.

JC   At that time we still weren't making coloured panels, so we did the printing with special inks.

TB   After creating this system we realized that we had another problem: with an almost transparent material on the façade, the heat insulation that was to cover the structure and ledges of the façade would be exposed.

JS   They asked us for an insulating material that would, on the one hand, withstand the high temperatures inside the air chamber in summer and, on the other, be satisfactory in appearance. From among our products, we chose an insulation made for air-conditioning ducts, which is covered with aluminium film and edged at the ends, which makes the pieces easier to join. Had they asked us to come up with a new product for this project we couldn't have done it, because the production would have been too limited. In one architectural project it is hard to generate enough critical mass for the development of new industrial products. We had to find a product we already had and adapt it to the specific needs of this project. When we talk about innovation we generally think of heavy investment with a complex, highly sophisticated organization, but innovation also lies in using existing materials in a different way.

TB We'd imagined an insulating material with a white face, which posed certain doubts about the colour concept. But the fact that the finish was silvery proved a great improvement on the reflective and chromatic quality of the façade.

FP If we had gone to the technology provider with a predetermined solution for the insulation, the result would surely have fallen short of our expectations. I believe that innovation occurs due to the interaction among all the parties involved in the building process.

JS And certainly the difficulty in finding people who understand each other is an obstacle to innovation and development in industry. I imagine that architects often deal with people who know a great deal about manufacturing, about the product they sell, but don't know a thing about construction. There has to a be certain common language, a minimum of points of contact, and the manufacturer must not only understand something about building but also be able to tell the architect: "we can take this road" or "if we take this road, the manufacturing process will be so complicated technologically that we'll stall out half way". I think the best example of the collaborative spirit we shared in the design of this façade is that the architects came to us with a problem, but they did not give us a solution.

FP Of course, there is also a basic personal component: we asked a specific technology provider, a specific manufacturer, who we had worked with before, and who didn't just advise us not to make things more difficult for ourselves.

JS In the end, innovations come from people. No company achieves anything on its own: it's the people behind it, the ones who understand that there is a problem to solve. And those people have the additional job of selling these innovations internally, within the company. Because the last thing a managing director or factory manager wants to do is try something that breaks with the norms...

FP And in this process of personal interaction the customer has a fundamental role. In this project we didn't have precedents or models we could show them, but still they agreed to go ahead with the project because they trusted in us and in our work. The processes of innovation are hard to justify on the balance sheet: they are largely the product of personal decisions.

JS In fact, in the building sector, innovation is seen as a risk rather than a virtue. It is hard to innovate because neither the buyer nor the innovator wants to take the gamble.

FP Surely we are part of the only productive sector where innovation is not a requirement for survival. Fortunately, it seems that this outlook is starting to change, to a large extent due to the need to meet environmental aspirations and regulations.

JS And also because innovation often pursues some sort of economic benefit, which in this case would come from the reduction in labour costs and the move to processes which are to a greater or lesser degree industrialized, and easily assembled.

FP The cost of this façade is very low, similar to that of a basic curtain wall like those that were built in the 1970s, but with very high performance. The savings comes from both the simplicity of construction and the small amount of material used. This savings evidently has a positive environmental impact.

TB The polycarbonate panels we used are fitted manually and, given that the material is so light-weight, the air vents in the inner chamber alone are enough to hold them in place, without the need for supplementary framework except for a few anchorings placed at different points of the structure to absorb the wind suction.

But I would like to point out that, in addition to its functionality and energy performance, this system of curtain wall has outstanding visual characteristics, based on the combination of a diffusive product, polycarbonate, and a reflective product, aluminium. Indeed, the façade produces two different effects from the outside and two others from the inside, depending on the time of day. This came as a surprise to us. We thought that during the day the colour would show, but instead it looks all white, with a wonderful shiny effect due to the reflectivity of the insulation.

Based on this experience we had the chance to further develop the system in a prototype we designed for the Casa Barcelona project, what we called the "green façade."

FP The Mediterranean curtain wall we built for this office building does not have thermal inertia, and that is what we set out to correct with the green façade. In order to achieve that, we filled the inner chamber with plants that provide this inertia (thus reducing the oscillations in temperature) and that also act as an evaporation-transpiration mechanism for the moisture of the roof and façade.

JS Today innovation in insulating products centres precisely on systems which take advantage of the change in state. The change from solid to liquid of any material requires heat input. The idea is to store this energy when there is an excess and then release it when you need it. In Arab courtyards there is always a surface of water which, in addition to its decorative function, lowers the ambient temperature through evaporation. This is the phenomenon we are pursuing in our research. We have to see what physical principles are behind these processes and how we can translate them into a contemporary architectural language.

I also think it is important to approach the question of energy savings and the environmental impact of buildings with a long-term vision and taking into account the manifold aspects that are associated with any decision. For example, thermal insulators not only save energy over the course of their life, but they also enable us to save water. If we measure the amount of water that is consumed in the production of the raw materials and the manufacture of the material, we will find that it is much less than what is needed to produce or transport the energy saved. We never use this sort of argument when we talk about savings and efficiency.

FP We should also take into account that in any construction there is material which is part of a cycle, that we can count as investment rather than as cost. The material used in one building can be recycled in another: it is used and assessed at the same time as an asset. I don't think it will be long before there are laws to require a certain percentage of recycled aggregates in cement manufacturing. Then we will look at the building under construction as the quarry for the building we'll be making 25 years down the road.

JS But let's not forget that a lightweight system like that used in this façade is a huge boost to the selective separation of the different materials used in it. In traditional construction, the brick sticks to the mortar and the mortar to the plaster, which makes the reuse of any of these materials enormously difficult. The concept of innovation in construction undoubtedly entails the use of components which are easy to separate.

Green façade

Architects Felipe Pich-Aguilera, Teresa Batlle (Pich-Aguilera Arquitectes)
Head of project Ute Müncheberg
Head of research Max Radt
Design team Pau Casaldàliga, Aurélie Lethu
Sponsors Fundación Rafael Escolá, Jon Laurenz Senosiain, Technal

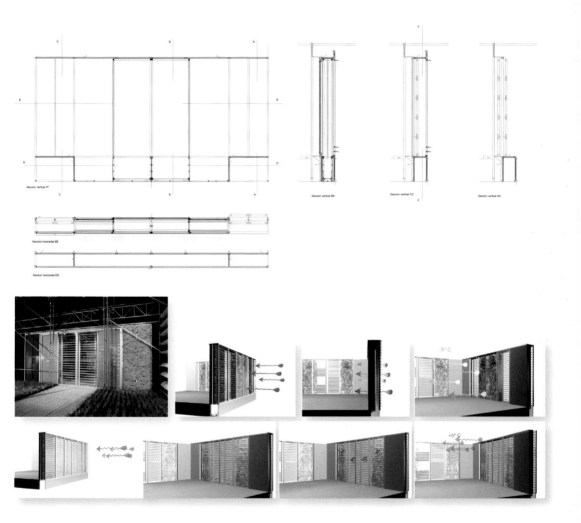

MEDITERRANEAN CURTAIN WALL
Office building for industrial and technological innovation activities (2004)

Location Carrer Àvila, Barcelona
Architects Felipe Pich-Aguilera, Teresa Batlle | www.picharchitects.com
Team directors Xavier Milanés, Ángel Sendarrubias
Project architect Margherita Aricó
Design team Ivan Acevedo Gómez, Ute Müncheberg, Aurélie Lethu
Interior design Lídia Manuseva
Sustainability consultant Emilio Mitre
Manufacturers Ramon Ros, Josep Solé (URSA), Joan Comí (GET), Manel Faura (Garcia-Faura)
Cost consultant Tecnics G3
Structural design BD Consultors / CYPE
M & E Engineering PGI
Photographs Toni Coll, Michel Roschach, Pich-Aguilera

Only the structure of the existing building is saved. The project includes a well-lit interior, where inner partitions are developed from flexible layouts that make interchangeable spaces possible according to different needs.
The new façade is divided in three layers based on bioclimatic criteria:
- An opaque ledge with an outer insulation and a silk-screen printed polycarbonate skin finish.
- A window strip made of a double glass aluminum framework.
- Double polycarbonate skin, silk-screen printed on its outside surface thatallows ventilation in its intermediate air chamber and thus generates convection and an improvement of the thermal conditions.
This new technological skin expresses the colors, textures and transparencies of the use and activity that takes place inside the building.

This façade is a revision of the traditional curtain wall, suitable for northern European countries, that responds to situations having little light and very low temperatures. But this image, when it is extrapolated to the Mediterranean, where there is excessive light and heat, irremediably involves obvious overheating and over exposure problems that must be solved with added machines and tools. Our intention was to think of a façade system that would have the transparency and lightness of the central European curtain wall but that would behave appropriately in our climatic context.

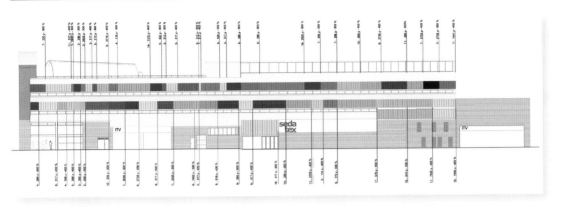

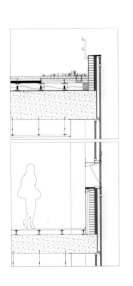

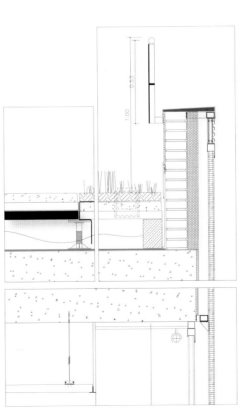

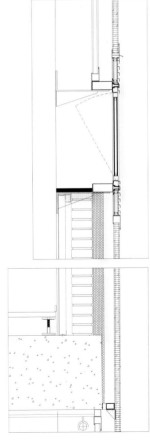

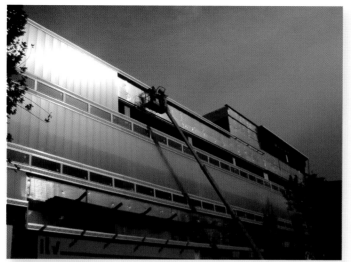

PERGOLA FAÇADE
House renovation (2005-2006)

Location Carrer Minerva, Barcelona
Architect Toni Gironès
Technical architect Sergi Pérez Cobos
Design team Susana Roque, Roger Mayol, Teresa Baldó
Steel construction Pidemunt
Wood construction De Tarima
Contractor Proyecto MYM60, SL
Photographs Toni Gironès

A narrow street. A program complimentary to the home: entrance through the garage, changing rooms, pool, and terrace...

An intention: from the emptiness of the inside of the block, a garden opens up to the city. We go through a reed panel and enter.

On the two floors (ground floor/garage + home/terrace), the continuous layout of programs was prioritized, as was their alternation and relationship at different seasons. The garage optimizes the useamount of space and mobility for two vehicles. The access to the terrace is located to the end of the lot, where natural light strengthens a certain continuity between the street and the garden space.

Natural cross ventilation and transparency condition the formal definition of the façade. Built with a main structure of corrugated steel (25 mm diameter), it is defined by its different densities, pressing the treated wood into a corrugated net (150 x 300 mm, diameter of 10 mm).

The free layout of the terrace offers a multi purpose space in continuity with the home.

The heated pool and greenery are located on the edge, on the main party wall, to achieve maximum depth. The steel and double wood screen in the shape of a pergola form the boundary of this space, and a small balcony allows the occasional relationship with the street, where the pedestrian will feel as approaching the reed screen of an old torrent rather than an urban construction.

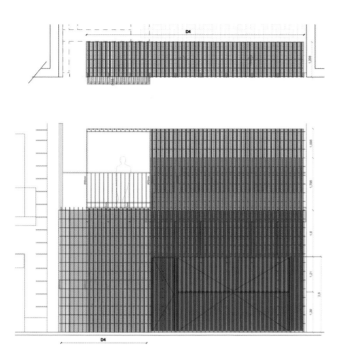

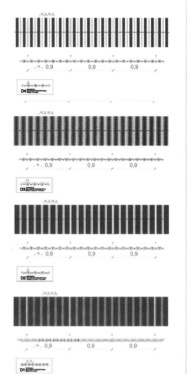

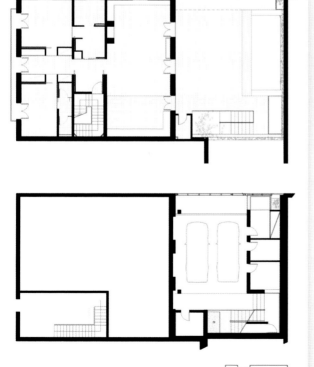

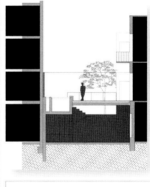

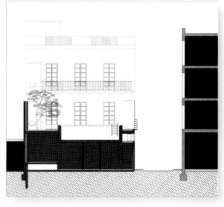

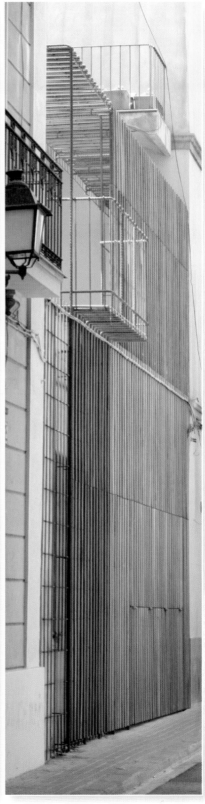

HABITAT

BREATHABLE HOUSE
Vineyard annex building, with access control, reception and miscellaneous activities (2003)

Location Tiana - Alella (Maresme)
Client Mas Igneus
Architect Alfons Soldevila Barbosa
http://arquitectes.coac.net/lacasatranslucida
Collaborating architect David Soldevila Riera
Contractor UNIVERSAL 88
Budget € 60,100
Floor area 95.57 m²

The commission is for a construction that contains three multipurpose spaces, able to house all the activities of the vineyard, including the control and reception of visitors.

A 6.5- by 28-metre rectangular enclosure is built of perforated brick, with the holes exposed so that one can see through it depending of the point of the view of the observer. At its corners, this enclosure is complemented by four reinforced concrete columns and a reinforced concrete ring which distributes the loads of the roof.

The roof does not cover the entire enclosure, leaving open-air front and rear patios. It is built of steel beams and ceramic vaults and a finish made from the same type of sandstone that is found in the soils of estate.

A second enclosure built within the first, with a separation of 60cm to one metre, defines the inhabitable space. This interior skin is made of brick rendered on the outer face and topped with a steel profile which keeps loads off the wall while resolving problems of weathertightness. Inside, the walls and ceiling are clad with a dry system of plasterboard substructure and sheets of painted or varnished MDF.

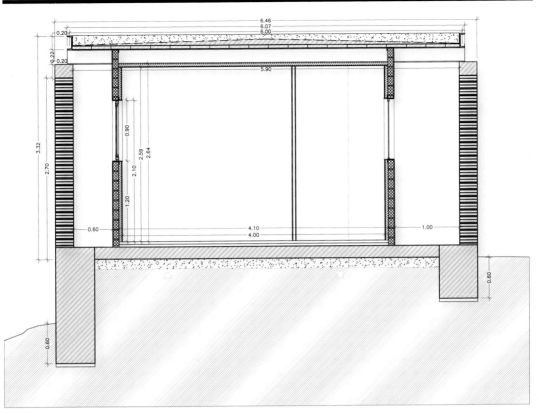

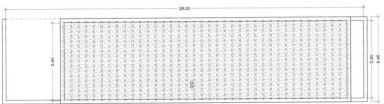

PLANTA COBERTA

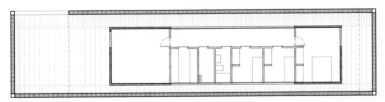

PLANTA BAIXA

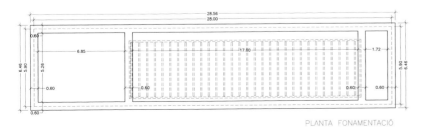

PLANTA FONAMENTACIÓ

·123·

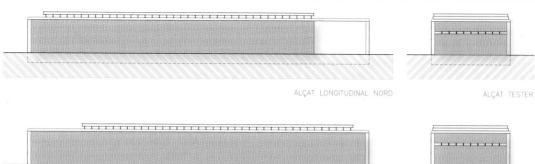

ALÇAT LONGITUDINAL NORD

ALÇAT TESTER

ALÇAT LONGITUDINAL

ALÇAT TESTER

GARDEN HOUSE
Villa Rosich (2002)

Location Igualada
Client Família Rosich
Architects Manuel Bailo + Rosa Rull (ADD+arquitectura) | www.addarquitectura.net
Project team J. Maroto, N. Canas, O. Florejachs, M. Hita, P. Juarez, A. Romero,
M. Rull, M. Cabestany, J. Vives
Budget € 300,000
Floor area 200 m²

This project fundamentally poses one question: how to build a house with a garden in a garden-city.

This is a house where the structure is intermingled with the garden through the construction of an ambivalent steel pergola. The load-bearing pergola frees the façade from the structure and allows the garden to enter the house. The house is designed to be unfinished, a garden-house that will continue to be built and change over time. With the construction of this pergola, the house is disassociated from its state of finished object, since it will be able to grow as a garden would.

The load-bearing structure is formed by a series of steel beams and pillars that are arranged in a longitudinal series across the plot. Of the six roof slabs, three are supported by the beams and the other three hang from them. This alternation in the ceiling height allows for daylight penetration and provides overhead views even in the innermost areas of the home.

The position of the brick walls that enclose the different spaces does not line up with the structural framework and roofs, thus generating indoor-outdoor transition spaces that enrich and singularize the relationship of the different indoor areas with the garden. The semi-manual brick used for the construction of these walls is laid with slight irregular shifts from the vertical plane, which generates a random vibration of light and shadows. Additionally, the interruption of the wall surface at certain points leaves the insulating panels made of oak cork exposed.

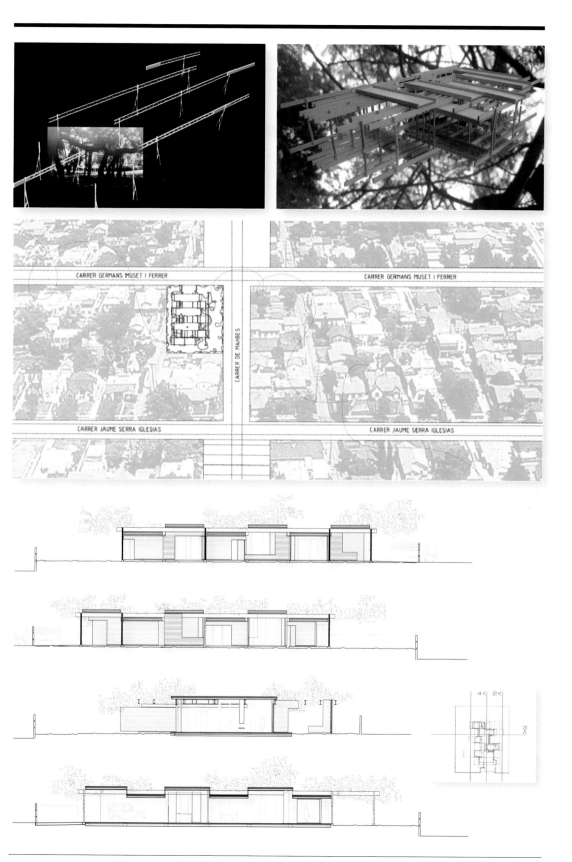

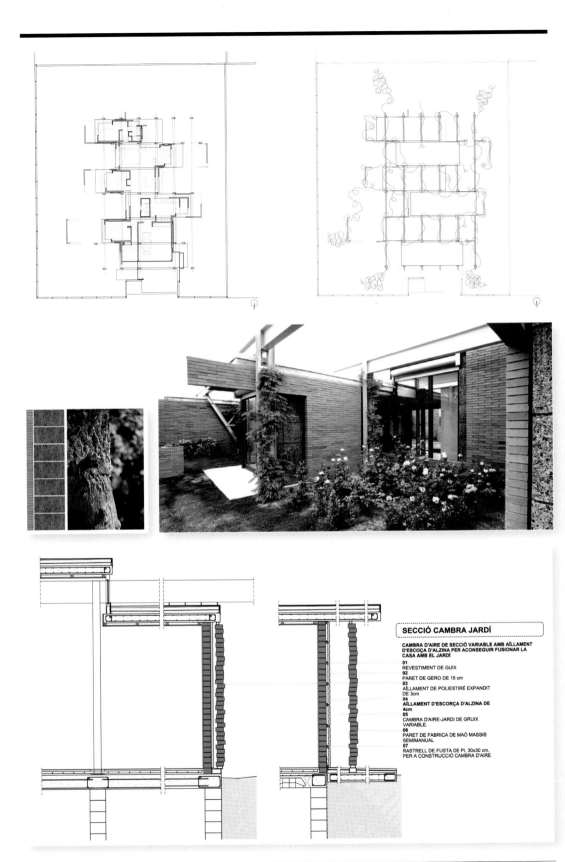

SECCIÓ CAMBRA JARDÍ

CAMBRA D'AIRE DE SECCIÓ VARIABLE AMB AÏLLAMENT
D'ESCOÇA D'ALZINA PER ACONSEGUIR FUSIONAR LA
CASA AMB EL JARDÍ

01
REVESTIMENT DE GUIX
02
PARET DE GERO DE 15 cm
03
AÏLLAMENT DE POLIESTIRÉ EXPANDIT
DE 3cm
04
AÏLLAMENT D'ESCORÇA D'ALZINA DE
4cm
05
CAMBRA D'AIRE-JARDÍ DE GRUIX
VARIABLE.
06
PARET DE FABRICA DE MAÓ MASSIS
SEMIMANUAL
07
RASTRELL DE FUSTA DE PI, 30x30 cm,
PER A CONSTRUCCIÓ CAMBRA D'AIRE

COOLING TOWER
Torre Cube (2002-2005)

Location Puerta de Hierro, Guadalajara (Mexico)
Client Cube Internacional
Architect Carme Pinós | www.cpinos.com
Design team Juan Antonio Andreu, Samuel Arriola, Frederic Jordan, César Vergés, Agustín Pérez, Holger Hennefarth, Caroline Lambrechts
Structural engineer Luis Bozzo
Site supervision Carme Pinós, Samuel Arriola
Contractor Anteus
Total floor area 7,000 m²
Photographs Duccio Malagamba, Lourdes Grobet

This project arises from the wish to create ventilated and well-lit offices, all the light being natural. We even ventured to think that air conditioning wouldn't be necessary, thanks to the good climate of the city of Guadalajara.

The structure comes from the breaking of the structural core normally found in the the center of office towers — containing facilities, stairwell, and elevator shaft — into three smaller cores or pillars. Large girders holding the floor slabs cantilever from these pillars, which make up the only vertical structure of the building. This structural system allows for the definition of open parking and office floors, free of obstacles. The center of the building, the space between the three pillars and vertical communication shafts, is an open space that is lit up sideways, alternatively eliminating three floors of office modules. The structure of the Torre Cube can be seen as if it were a tree: a balanced trunk and branches. The light penetrates the entire building in the way it would be filtered by foliage, and transforms the color of the structure at different times of day. The empty space of the center allows for cross ventilation and sliding doors of wood lattice in front of the operable windows create brises soleil.

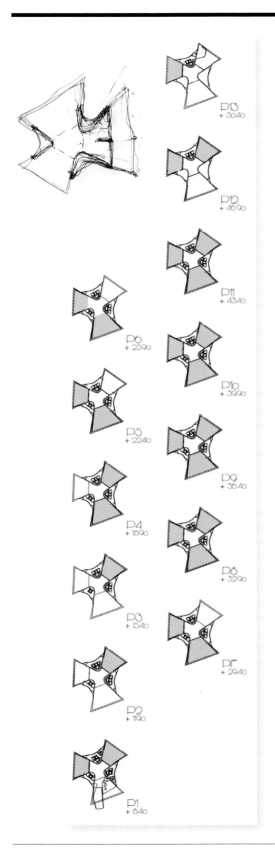

P13
+ 50.40

P12
+ 46.90

P11
+ 43.40

P6
+ 25.90

P10
+ 39.90

P5
+ 22.40

P9
+ 36.40

P4
+ 18.90

P8
+ 32.90

P3
+ 15.40

P7
+ 29.40

P2
+ 11.90

P1
+ 8.40

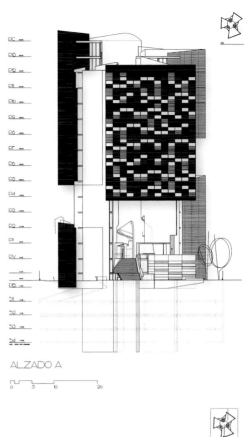

ALZADO A

0   5   10   20

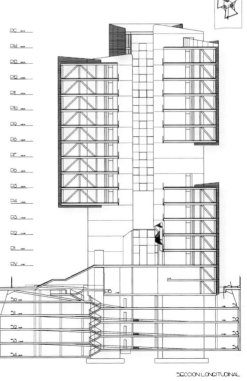

SECCION LONGITUDINAL

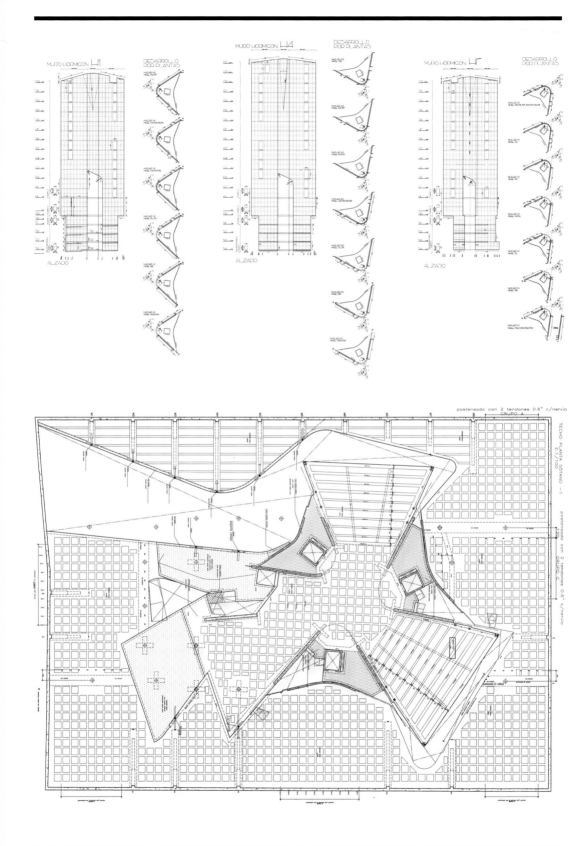

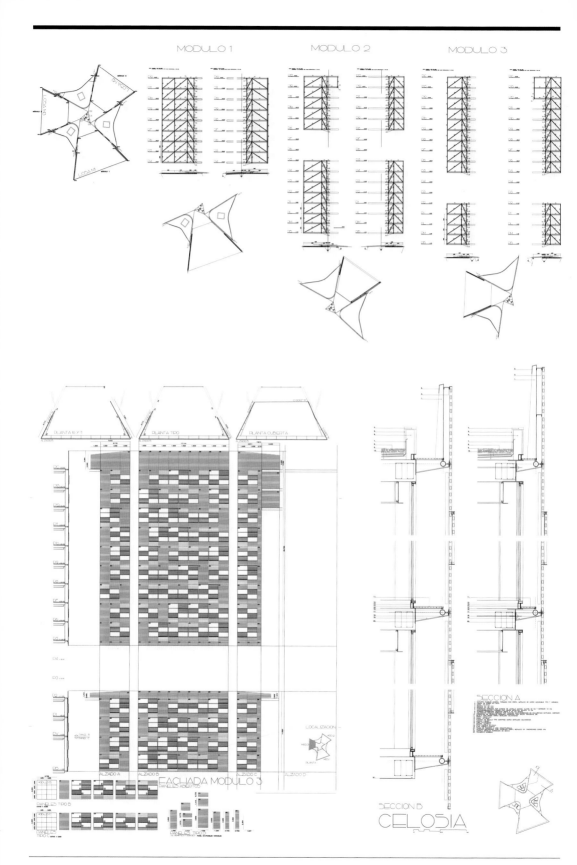

MODULO 1   MODULO 2   MODULO 3

FACHADA MODULO 3

SECCION A

SECCION B

CELOSIA

TENT-MUSEUM
Huarte Art Center (2003-2007)

Location Huarte, Navarra
Client The City of Huarte
Architects FFPV Arquitectura | www.ffpvarquitectura.com
Franc Fernández , Carles Puig, Xavi Vancells
Design team Xavier Tutó, Carolina Jarreta, David Batllés, Raul Salas, Teresa Giménez
Structural design Base Dos Estructuras
Engineering RC Enginyers
Contractor UTE Brues y Fernández Construcciones SA – Gesai SA
Developer Sociedad Municipal de Gestión Urbanística AREACEA
Total floor area 6,154 m²
Photography Andrés Flajszer

We see the new Huarte Art Center as a social activity and exhibition center that can be expanded, modified, or restructured permanently. Under these premises, the design strategy generates spaces for a diversity of exhibits and activities in the building, emphasizing that the important part of the museum is its activity and NOT the building itself.

The building is defined not only by the content displayed inside, but also by the changing activity that is carried out in its surroundings: open air films, temporary outdoor exhibits, musical performances, celebrations, and public events. These events happen, thus creating active interaction between museum, city, and natural surroundings.

From this strategy a series of spaces are defined:

1. The lower space. The building hangs over a new recessed topography that generates a parking area that can host different activities depending on time and season.

2. The encircling space. The building is wrapped around itself by means of the faceted geometry of a tensed steel net that defines a series of green spaces around it, spaces prepared to host temporary outdoor exhibits as well as different official and social events.

3. The platform space. The ground level of the set is designed as a highly permeable transparent public level that regulates different entrances to the building, allowing independent use of spaces at different times.

4. The exhibition space: Empty, neutral spaces with the proper facilities and infrastructures for changing with each exhibit or performance serving as a large theatre.

The art center becomes a focal point of activities that encourages participation in the public life of Huarte.

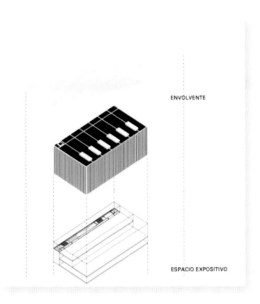

ENVOLVENTE

ESPACIO EXPOSITIVO

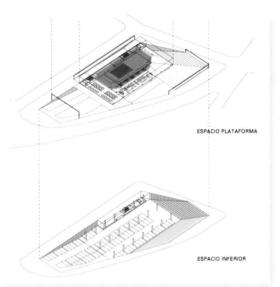

ESPACIO PLATAFORMA

ESPACIO INFERIOR

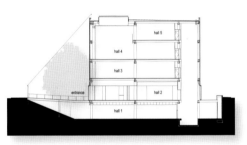

hall 5

hall 4

hall 3

entrance

hall 2

hall 1

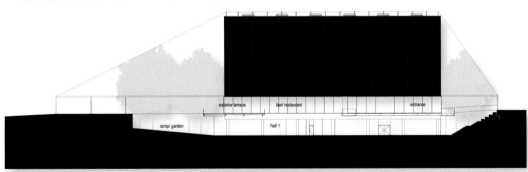

exterior terrace   bar/ restaurant   entrance

ramp/ garden   hall 1

0   5   10   15

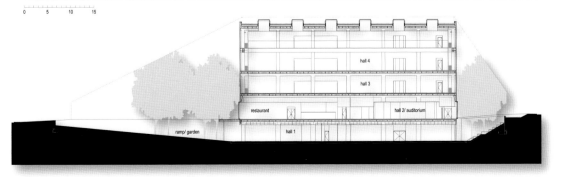

hall 4

hall 3

restaurant   hall 2/ auditorium

ramp/ garden   hall 1

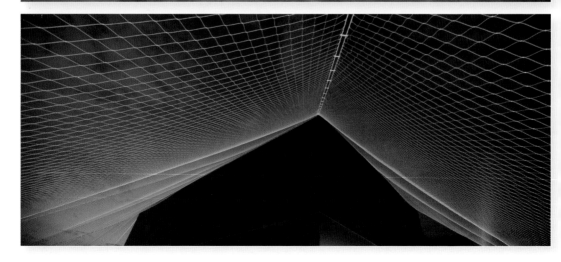

PERMEABLE BLOCK
Mixed-use building: 45 housing units, primary school and kindergarten (2001-2006)

Location Carrer Londres / Carrer Villarroel, Barcelona
Client Ajuntament de Barcelona - Proeixample
Architects Jaime Coll, Judith Leclerc | www.coll-leclerc.com
Structural engineer Manuel Arguijo
M&E engineering JSS
Landscape architect Teresa Galí
Cost consultant Xavier Badia
Project manager GPO
Design team Odon Esteban, Urtzi Grau, Adrià Goula, Jordi Giralt, Ema Dünner, Eduard Rosignol, Thomas Kenniff, Narcís Font, Mireia Martinez, Aurora Leon, Jacob Hense, Tomeu Ramis, Cristian Vivas, Phillipe Coudeau, José Ulloa
Contractor FCC
Total floor area 22,187 m²
Budget € 11,537,447
Photographs José Hevia

The competition brief divided the lot in two parts — the north-facing chamfered corner, lacking sunlight and ventilation, to build homes around 40 m² for young people, and an elongated area facing the street, to build an early education and primary school, whose floor area ratio was much higher than the one required. Our proposal brought back an unfrequently used typology in the Eixample of Barcelona, the "Mediterráneo" buildings by Antonio Bonet, a hybrid that did not seek so much to break Cerdà's rules, but to explore the true potential of those ordinances that were never passed that allowed the standardization of accidents as a regular component, not an exception, of the grid system; alleys, ground-floor workshops, patios on façades, unorthogonal intersections, etc.

Our project also explores the idea of the permeable block that is at the origin of the Eixample. The street extends its 20 meter width with a series of parallel spaces, a bar code where the strips rub against each other, alternating empty and full spaces, light and construction, and create visual relationships and transversal connections between street and inner block.

The project takes up the available 28.5 meter depth dividing the buildings in narrow, parallel volumes, staggered from north to south and thus allows the sunlight to reach both homes and classrooms. It causes two different programs (school and home) to coexist and relate to each other. Between these two programs there is a passage or entrance patio to the school which decongests the sidewalks of the masses of students that generally concentrate at schools' entrances.

The proposal thus suggests a reclassification of the entrances, circulation, and open spaces (patios, balconies, decks) that become spaces of relationship and exchange, with sunlight and ventilation. The whole works like a miniature city.

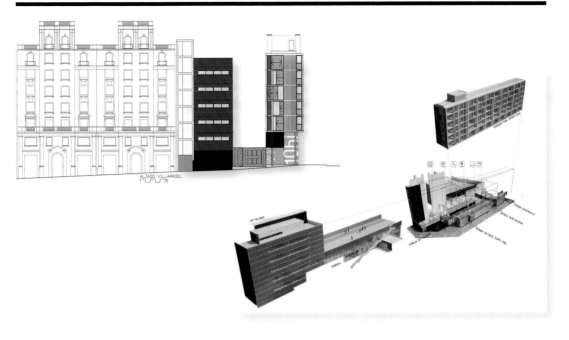

ALZADO VILLARROEL

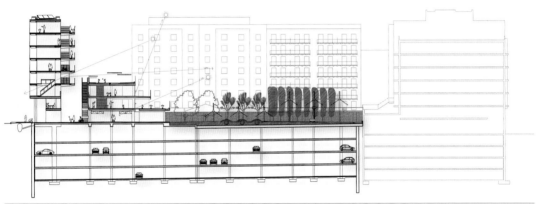

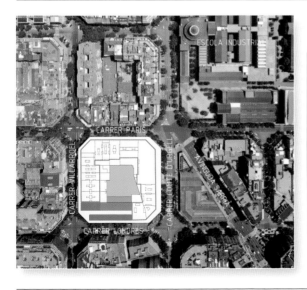

ESCOLA INDUSTRIAL

CARRER PARIS

CARRER VILLARROEL

CARRER COMTE D'URGELL

AVINGUDA ROMA

CARRER LONDRES

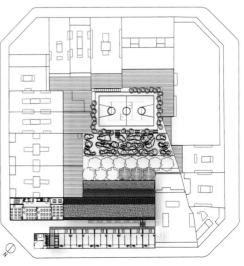

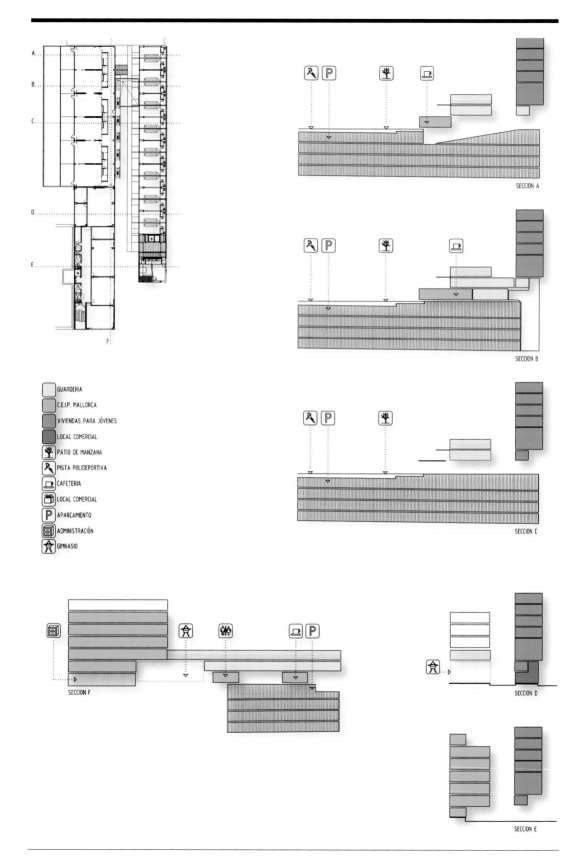

GUARDERIA

C.E.I.P. MALLORCA

VIVIENDAS PARA JÓVENES

LOCAL COMERCIAL

PATIO DE MANZANA

PISTA POLIDEPORTIVA

CAFETERIA

LOCAL COMERCIAL

APARCAMIENTO

ADMINISTRACIÓN

GIMNASIO

SECCION A

SECCION B

SECCION C

SECCION D

SECCION E

SECCION F

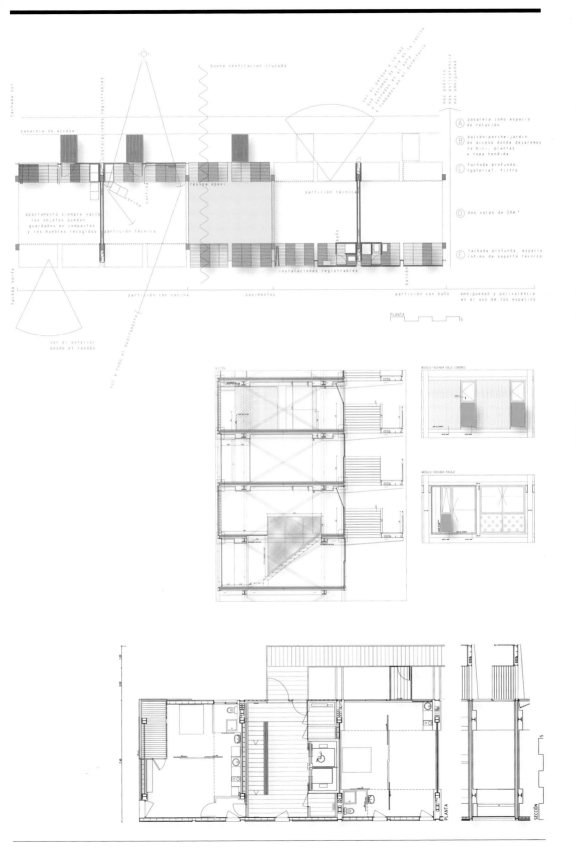

EXTERIOR INTERIOR
Building with 34 apartments (2001-2004)

Location Cambrils
Architects Vicente Guallart and María Diaz | www.guallart.com
Design team Barbara Oelbrant, Pilar Basque, Cristina Dorado
Models Christine Bleicher
Glass Cricursa
Steel Masdeu
Developer Inmondial S.L. Pellicer y Fills S.A.
Photographs Laura Cantarella

The buildings, having a square floor plan, are designed according to new spatial and functional organizations with the goal of benefitting from the seaside condition of the plot. One of the specific factors developed is the relationship of the rooms with the large terrace around them, conceived to literally expand the space of each apartment. By means of folding doors or curtains, the terraces become fundamental circulation spaces, physically extending the rooms towards the outside. The kitchen and bathrooms face the outside. The sea can be seen from the bathrooms.

The construction of such a transparent façade in an apartment building required the definition of a second skin that would guarantee a certain degree of privacy. Colored glass could provide this protection while also interacting with the landscape, very beautiful but also marked by scattered development. We decided to create a gradation of colors that responded to the views and sun exposure. The result is an image based on rhythms: the aluminum on the façade is related to its function and reflects its surroundings, while the light glass skin defines a protective veil.

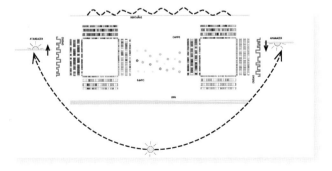

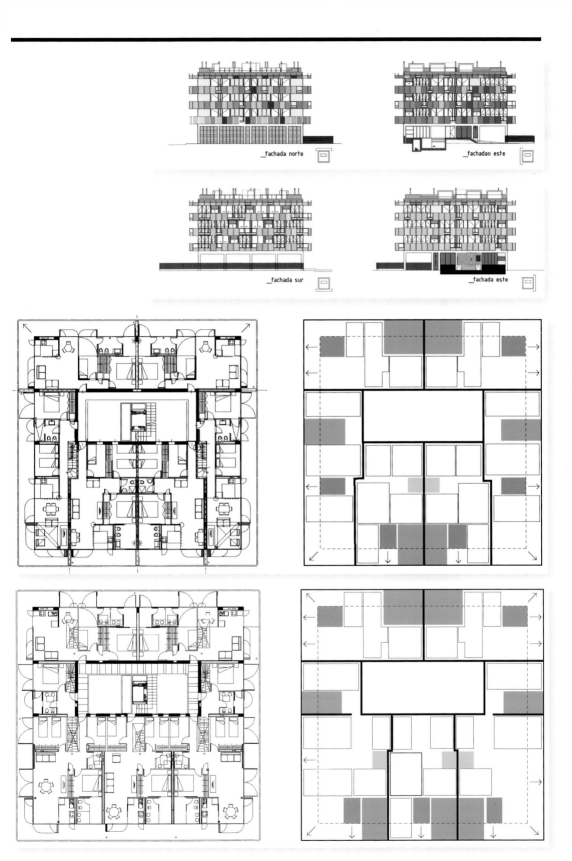

_fachada norte

_fachadao este

_fachada sur

_fachada este

SPIRAL SPACE
Villa Bio (2002-2005)

Location Llers (Alt Empordà)
Client Familia Fontecha
Main architect Enric Ruiz Geli - Cloud 9 | www.e-cloud9.com | www.ruiz-geli.com
Interior design Manel Soler Caralps
Design team Frederic Guillard, Andre Brösel, Oscar Puga (Cloud 9)
Engineer Manel Raventós
Technical architect Arantza Garetaonandia
Structural engineering Antonio Diosdado
M&E engineering Joaquim Ribes Quintana, Toni Jordà
Contractors Joaquim Quirante, Industrias Bec, Solatube, Ecoextractores
Landscaping Joan Madorell

Glass Cricursa	**Green roof** Jardines Burés
Events Emiliana Design Estudio	**Mobile partitions** Panalite
Window frames Aluminis Empordà	**Fixed partitions** Japlac, Vetroarredo
Graphic design Laia Jutglà	**Kitchen furniture** Samaniego
Floors Pavindus, SA	**Paint** Noucolor
Waterproofing Roure i Pujol	**Lighting** Iguzzini
Concrete molding Valchromat	**Photographs** Ramon Prat, Gunnar Knechtel

Contemporary architecture is the platform of contemporary art and culture.
Living is an existing platform that can become an art form: the art of living.
We conceive this platform as a linear landscape of events.
This landscape is folded to form a growing spiral.
The platform is a linear concrete structure with a constant C-shaped cross-section.
The blind longitudinal façades function as beams and cantilever 15 meters.
Concrete is a liquid material that solidifies and thus creates a liquid topography on the façade.

Process:
1. We created a three-dimensional model of the topographical landscape that we wished to construct.
2. A Virilian landscape of accidents.
3. By CAD/CAM process with CNC milling machine, we shaped a personalized, unique and non-standard 24 by 3 meter image.
4. We treated the mold and turned it into the formwork of the north and south longitudinal façades.

The platform liquifies and mutates, covered by a roof garden, an inner landscape of glass (stone) with digital rendering plotters...
BIO architecture.

© patent in process

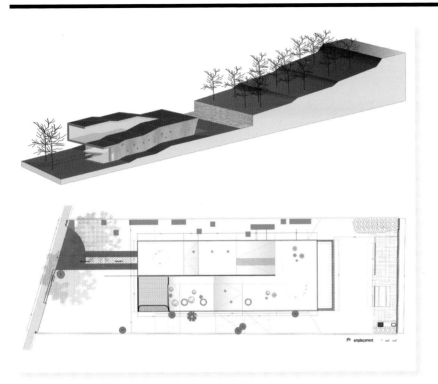

emplaçament

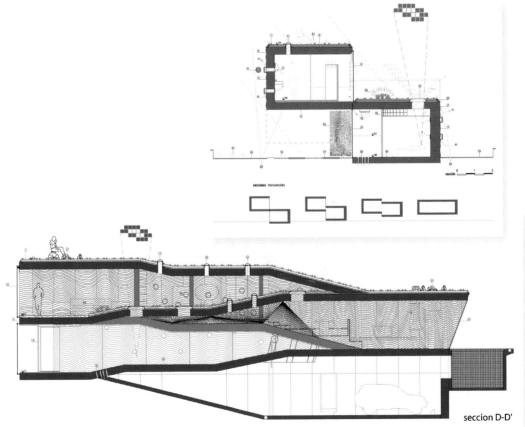

seccioes transversales

seccion D-D'

INTIMATE GLASS
Sleeping pavilions at the
Restaurant Les Cols (2002-2005)

Location Olot
Client Joaquim Puigdevall - Judit Planella
Architects RCR: Rafael Aranda, Carme Pigem, Ramon Vilalta | www.rcrarquitectes.es
Project collaborators M. Subiràs (Project), A. Sáez (Structure), M. Subiràs, M. Marques (Project leaders), I. De Vasconcelos (Model), V. Hannotin, F. Spratley (Visualization)
Contractor Joaquim Puigdevall
Surface Area 130 m²
Budget € 110,000
Photography Eugeni Pons

This brief asked for a night rest area next to the restaurant Les Cols. The site is an isolated plot that surrounds the Les Cols country estate like an oasis in the city.

With the structure of the gardens, strips of land protected by walls of green, these spaces are generated out of partial coverings. Among these coverings are the high walls that protect them along a descending path, where the sight and pleasure of the night sky acquires an essential prominence. For a night of rest, the project proposes a way of living: finding oneself alone against the night and void, sheltered inside warm walls, where the opaque and the reflection of sheet glass are combined in a rich play of light and water, causing one to feel once again aspects of nature that had been forgotten about.

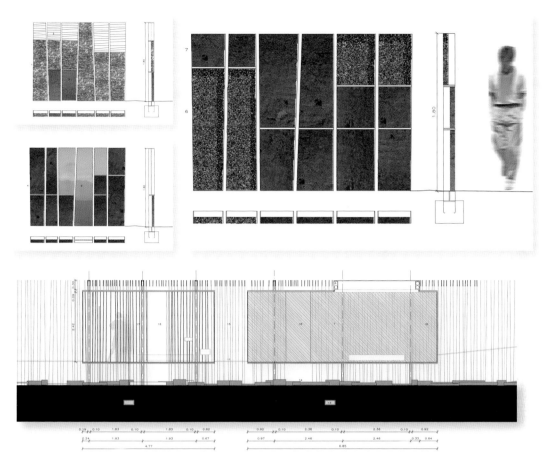

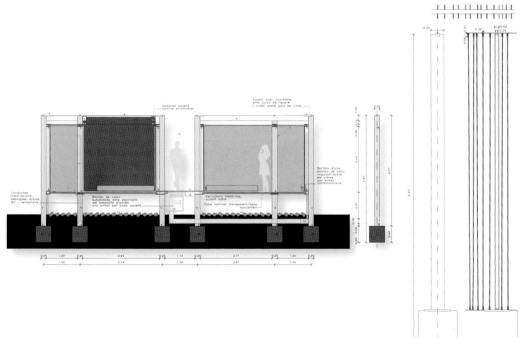

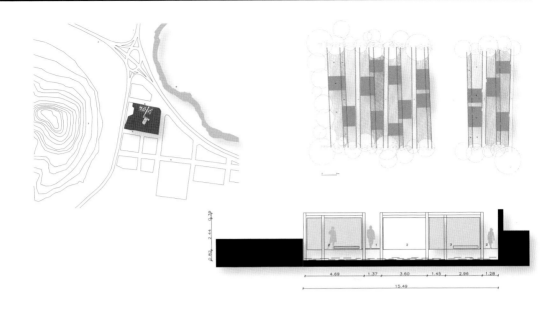

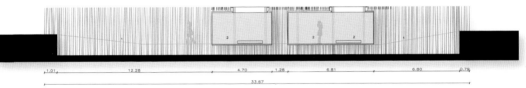

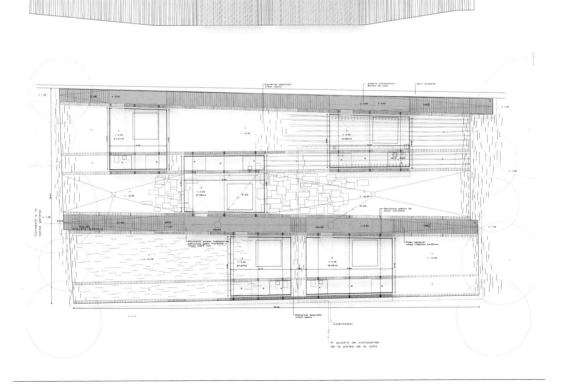

ONE TABLE, THREE POSITIONS (EXHIBITION-SUPPER-PARTY)
Stage direction of Laus Night 06 (2006)

Location Teatre Mercat de les Flors. Barcelona
Client ADG FAD
Arquitectos BOPBAA. Josep Bohigas, Francesc Pla, Iñaki Baquero
Collaborators Laura López Fuentes, Francoise Boujou
Audiovisuals BOOLAB
Graphic Design Dani Navarro
Installation La Central de Projectes, Equip tècnic del Mercat de les Flors

Laus Night is a graphic design, advertising and audio-visuals exhibition and awards ceremony organized each year by the ADG FAD association. For 2006, the project brief set out several programmes over the course of the evening: an exhibition of the finalist projects for the prizes (100), dinner (500 people), the awards ceremony and a party. The space chosen was a theatre, the Mercat de les Flors. The aim of the project was to exploit fully all the resources and infrastructures of the theatre, using the equipment as well as the language and the technicians who usually work there.

The first decision of the project was to invert the natural position of the stage, turning the tiered seating into the audio-visual project space and awards ceremony stage. The public, on the other hand, was located on what is normally the stage, facing the seating, beneath the stage machinery, thus becoming the real stars of the evening.

From the ceiling were suspended 24 triple-ply cardboard tables with full place settings – cutlery, plates, glassware, food, wine, dessert etc – ready to be lowered for immediate dining. From below, no one saw them...

In their original position, the tables were at mid elevation and the triangulations of the legs generated an illuminated drop ceiling which was the support for the exhibition of the graphic works of the finalists.

People entered, and browsed the exhibition while having an aperitif, until an audio-visual advised of the lowering of the tables. A minute later, the 500 people were seated around the set tables, the food served and glass of wine in hand.

An instantaneous supper which avoided the tricky movement of servers among so many people, and which, like a curtain, marked the start of the event.

Over the next hour, supper was eaten and the prizes awarded, after which the tables rose once again (this time up to the ceiling) to leave the space free for the party.

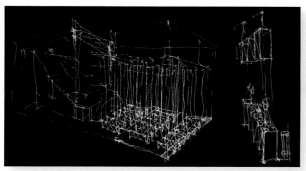

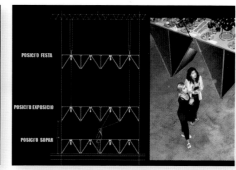

POSICIÓ FESTA

POSICIÓ EXPOSICIÓ

POSICIÓ SOPAR

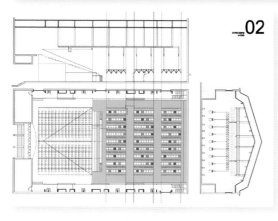

02

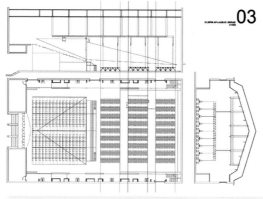

03

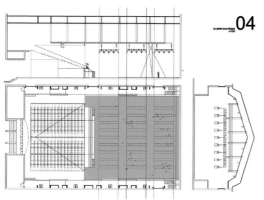

04

LANDSCAPE

LANDSCAPE OBJECTS
EP: Enric Pericas, Escofet
MF: Makoto Fukuda

MF   I would like to talk about the collaboration among architects and industrialists, about innovation as well as tradition as I think that Catalonia has always had a tendency to create new and original forms. This is the situation that I experienced in the design process of Lungo Mare, where I worked with EMBT (Enric Miralles + Benedetta Tagliabue). I have the impression that in Lungo Mare there was a rediscovery of the grammar of landscaping applied to public space, as a versatile element we can sit, lean, lie, or play on.

EP   Lungo Mare indeed marks a point of departure, a new way of conceiving urban furniture. Until then, no one had worked under those parameters in the field of public spaces. Escofet began producing urban furniture in the 1970s, which coincided with the end of Franco's regime and the reinstatement of democratic municipal governments, a moment when architects became completely involved in the design of public space, of urban landscape. But the elements that Escofet edited before Lungo Mare couldn't build a landscape since they had a more generic use. The perception that Lungo Mare produced in the year 2000, when its use began, was so innovative that it was taken to be a sculpture. In fact, you designed a space, a place, where each person could find his or her place, and it wasn't anything more than a fragment of a beach that had been installed in a new place, firstly in the Diagonal Mar park.

MF   There are elements, like a stone or a trunk, that are perfectly appropriate for sitting in the city. But in a park, you can think of other types of elements that allow not just for sitting, but for other positions as well. This was our approach then.

EP   I think that public space demands quite specific projects according to the scale of the intervention: some scales allow complex forms and others do not. When you consider the pavement of a pedestrian street, the project is practically limited to a manipulation of the outer layers: pavement, tree gratings, and street lights. But when you work in a space on a larger scale like in metropolitan parks, you must be capable of generating installations that are ambitious and original. You have to think of something new, something capable of creating a landscape.

MF   If we work on an architectural project, we always think about landscaping or urban planning as well. And in this type of urban installations, I think you have to figure out how to operate between landscape and use, between the public sphere of the city and the private sphere of the inhabitant. I live in Barcelona and Tokyo, where the gradation between public and private is very different. Catalonia is more open to dissolving the limits between these two areas.

EP   Because here there is an urban culture that is shared by the administration and the people. The proof can be seen whenever a public square is built in Barcelona and people go to see it and test it, the news comes out in newspapers. There is a large public involvement and this is a part of our culture that has been forged over the years. People expect that important projects for the city will be something new, something interesting, and something innovative.

MF   I suppose that this is what happened with the Diagonal Mar park, a project that contributed to the definition of a new urban development. The design process began with a series of photographs and photo montages of the beach, which guided us all the way like a map would. On the beach there was a broken chair with no one on it facing the sea. We sat down on the sand next to it. Then looking at the waves and the pattern of the sand, we began to conceive that wavy shape. I think that many people have dreamed at some point that they were sitting on the sea, as on a flying carpet. We started to create models from that simple concept, cutting wood and alternating between different scales. My model was the Chaise Longue by Le Corbusier and Charlotte Perriand. Her figure leaning there was perfect. I cut it out and used it as a model. Escofet then directed us to a workshop that produces art nouveau ornaments in plaster, where there was a great craftsman. I think that people who are dedicated to these type of traditions should also take part in this kind of innovation. There I began to manipulate the model, to adapt it to the different positions that I defined with my own body. Studying the different positions of the body on a computer was still complicated.

EP In spite of being an innovative idea, Lungo Mare was built with very classical technology, completely out of date if we compare it to what we use now, with 3D files that are directly placed on a model in six, eight, or 24 hours using a CNC milling machine. From that model we create a mold. Lungo Mare and Naguisa, the element designed recently by Toyo Ito and that you also worked in, are related products in concept but very different in their production process. All that craftsman experience can be reproduced in a faster, more economical, and more efficient way using digital technology. Now we could have produced several models of Lungo Mare and we could have built them in different places around the world from the same digital archive. This was formerly unimaginable, because the production required a plaster model.

MF I still think that Lungo Mare was a more complex element, that could not be controlled ergonomically in 3D with the same precision as the traditional system that we used. Architecture and design now have new technology at their disposal but we also have old technology. Our work alwas looks for the possibility of innovation but the source of innovation also lies in activity.

EP Today we could have obtained the same level of control, or even higher, in a 3D model. In the end, this bench doesn't have to respond to your body, but to everyone's body. We always say that people both large and small could fit there just as well, all just as comfortable as the others. In Lungo Mare, all possible sections are there. Enric Miralles said that when you left Lungo Mare, you left the trace of your body. I think, as you say, that the most innovative aspect of this element is the type of activity it generates, the way of understanding the action of the user. Nowadays, urban elements are more open, less predefined, so as to generate an interaction with the users. A chair is something that has a definition: it is to sit on and that's it. But this new generation of urban elements is not just to be sat on, but to stimulate a person who comes before them to react. I think we have recovered that capacity that Gaudí or Pere Falqués could use in the streetlight-benches of the Passeig de Gràcia which is that symbolic value of identity.

ROOF GARDEN
Renovation of the
Santa Caterina Market (1997-2005)

Location Av. Francesc Cambó, Barcelona
Client Foment de Ciutat Vella S.A.
Architects Enric Miralles, Benedetta Tagliabue (EMBT) | www.mirallestagliabue.com
Project team Igor Peraza (director de proyecto), Hirotaka Koizuni, Josep Miàs,
Marta Cases, Constanza Chara, Eugenio Cirulli, Santiago Crespi, Gianfranco Grondona,
Lluis Corbella, Massimo Chizzola, Joan Poca, Alejandra Vazquez, Marco Dario Chirdel,
Josep Belles. Alicia Bramon, Laura Valentini, Adelaide Passetti, Jorge Carvajal, Andrea Landell
de Moura, Torsten Skoetz, Karl Unglaub, Adrien Verschuere, Loïc Gestin, Annie Marcela Henao,
Ezequiel Cattaneo, Leonardo Giovannozzi, Annette Hoeller, Sabine Bauchmann, Silke Techen,
Barbara Oel Brandt, Mette Olsen, Florencia Vetcher, Nils Becker, Raphael de Montard,
Montse Galindo, Barbara Appolloni, Jean François Vaudeville, Peter Sándor Nagy,
Ignacio Quintana, Christian Molina, Stefan Geenen, Maarten Vermeiren, Torsten Schmid,
Joan Callís, Ane Ebbeskov Olsen, Dani Rosselló, Francesco Mozzati, Francesco Jacques-Dias,
Fernanda Hannah, Elena Rocchi, Makoto Fukuda, Ricardo Flores, Eva Prats, Fabián Asunción,
German Zambrana, Lluís Cantallops, Anna Maria Tosi, Marc Forteza Parera, Anna Galmer,
Liliana Bonforte, Tobias Gottschalk, Stefan Eckert, Ute Grölz, Thomas Wuttke, Luca Tonella,
Stéphanie Le Draoullec, Monica Carrera (EMBT)
Structure Robert Brufau
Engineering José María Velasco (roof), Miquel Llorens (housing)
Ceramic Ceràmica Cumella
M&E engineering PGI
Contractor COMSA
Photographs Alex Gaultier, EMBT

Ciutat Vella, unlike other neighborhoods in Barcelona, is a complete city. Perhaps this is the clearest quality of historical centers. From this point on, things get more complicated. The existing masterplan for the renovation of the area cannot manage the complexity of the situation and in wanting to be immediately effective, it unbearably simplifies the rules of the game.

The first mistake is thinking we can talk about old versus new. The constructed form has a complex relationship with time. Anything that has survived up to today is current, useful, and contemporary. It also allows you to go back in time in order to go forward. Another mistake is defending tearing things down as the only way to "solve" problems. On the contrary: use and reuse.

In this way new construction is placed on top of existing structures. They are mixed and confused to make that place seem to be at the height of its existence... It so seems logical to use words like conglomerate, hybrid, etc., words that attempt to go beyond a simple division between black and white. Overlapping different movements in time offers spectacular possibilities. It gives way to a play on differences.

We propose a model where it is not so easy to distinguish between renovation and new construction, where continuity travels down the street as the only definition mechanism of urban form, contributing public space and residential density.

The roof unifies the perimeter of the market and is the defining element of the new public space. With the design of the ceramic surface of the roof we wished to represent the colors of the typical produce of Mediterranean markets.

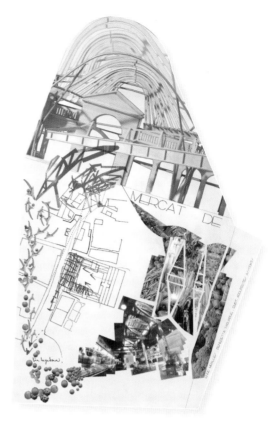

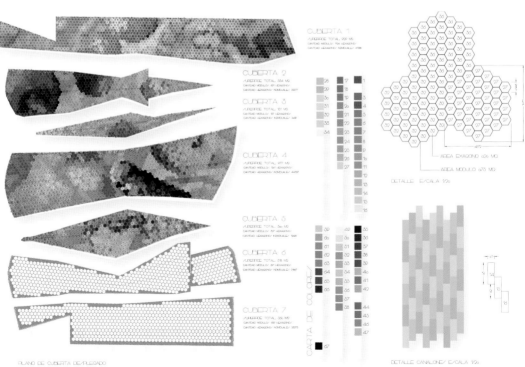

CUBERTA 1
SUPERFICIE TOTAL: 509 M2
CANTIDAD MODULOS: 756 HEXAGONOS
CANTIDAD HEXAGONOS MODULO: 4738

CUBERTA 2
SUPERFICIE TOTAL: 334 M2
CANTIDAD MODULOS: 89 HEXAGONOS
CANTIDAD HEXAGONOS MODULO: 2977

CUBERTA 3
SUPERFICIE TOTAL: 101 M2
CANTIDAD MODULOS: 87 HEXAGONOS
CANTIDAD HEXAGONOS MODULO: 348

CUBERTA 4
SUPERFICIE TOTAL: 977 M2
CANTIDAD MODULOS: 134 HEXAGONOS
CANTIDAD HEXAGONOS MODULO: 4637

CUBERTA 5
SUPERFICIE TOTAL: 366 M2
CANTIDAD MODULOS: 89 HEXAGONOS
CANTIDAD HEXAGONOS MODULO: 1949

CUBERTA 6
SUPERFICIE TOTAL: 578 M2
CANTIDAD MODULOS: 89 HEXAGONOS
CANTIDAD HEXAGONOS MODULO: 2147

CUBERTA 7
SUPERFICIE TOTAL: 355 M2
CANTIDAD MODULOS: 88 HEXAGONOS
CANTIDAD HEXAGONOS MODULO: 1873

CARTA DE COLOR

AREA EXAGONO: 0.05 M2

AREA MODULO: 0.70 M2

DETALLE ESCALA 1/20

PLANO DE CUBERTA DESPLEGADO

DETALLE CANALONES ESCALA 1/20

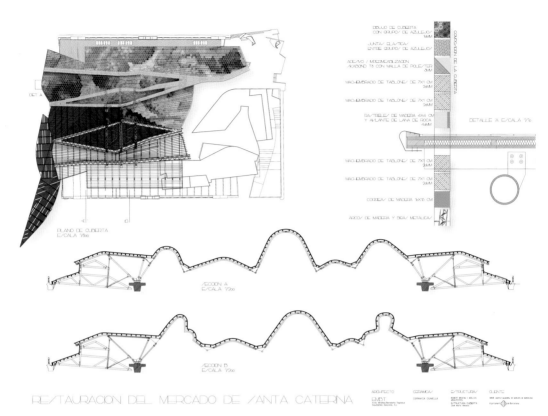

POOL WALK
Intervention to a private garden: lookout, storage/fitness room and swimming-pool (2004-2005)

Location Jafre (Alt Empordà)
Clients Joan Descalç, Rosa Martín
Architects Jordi Hidalgo, Daniela Hartmann | www.hidalgohartmann.com
Design team Ana Roque, Rafel Serra
Structure Cota21
Swimming-pool Filjod SA
Technical architect Joel Vives
Contractor Ribera Soy SL
Budget € 72,500
Surface 382 m2
Photography Robert Prat Riera, Jordi Hidalgo

This intervention is located on the plain of l'Empordà, with its characteristic vast extensions of agricultural field scattered with wooden areas.

A swimming pool, a storage space for garden utensils, and the creation of an entrance for both were the elements of the brief. The design of each of these three elements is integrated into one single spatial experience, one block inserted in the landscape — which is modified and redefined.

Its outline triggers the image of dirt paths and the meandering of rivers that, in their formal freedom, highlight their difference from the geometric rigidness of the fields.

The pool, stretching transversely accross the garden in the direction of the Montgrí mountain, is perceived as a plane anchored to the land by means of a path that connects the different levels of the garden.

The volume containing the underground storage space is located at the point of highest vertical drop, and accessed via a long concrete ramp ending in a discontinuous and irregular pavement made up of circular concrete circles.

From a hardly visible crease in the land, the structure is folded in an act of constant escape, forming an elevated viewing platform.

Beginning at a wall, the spatial experience is a complex assemblage of planes that flows into the projecting pool, where the water pours into the earth as a waterfall.

The presence of concrete as a single material emphasizes the abstract nature of the object.

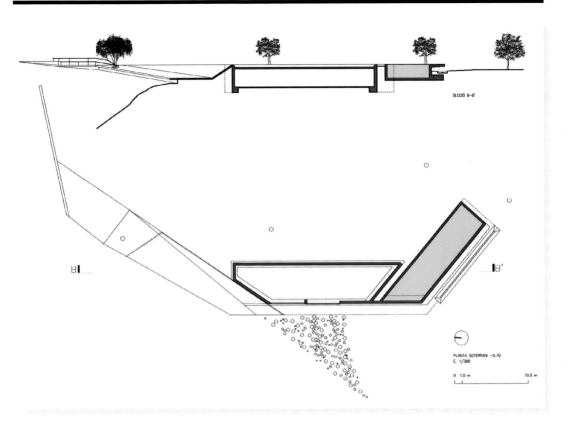

SECCIÓ B-B'

PLANTA SOTERRANI -0.70
E. 1/300

0   1.0 m   10.0 m

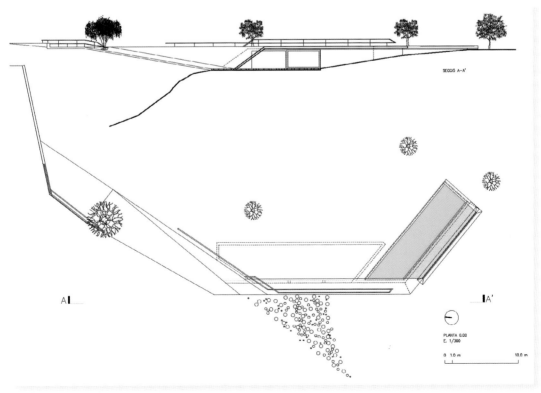

SECCIÓ A-A'

PLANTA 0.00
E. 1/300

0   1.0 m   10.0 m

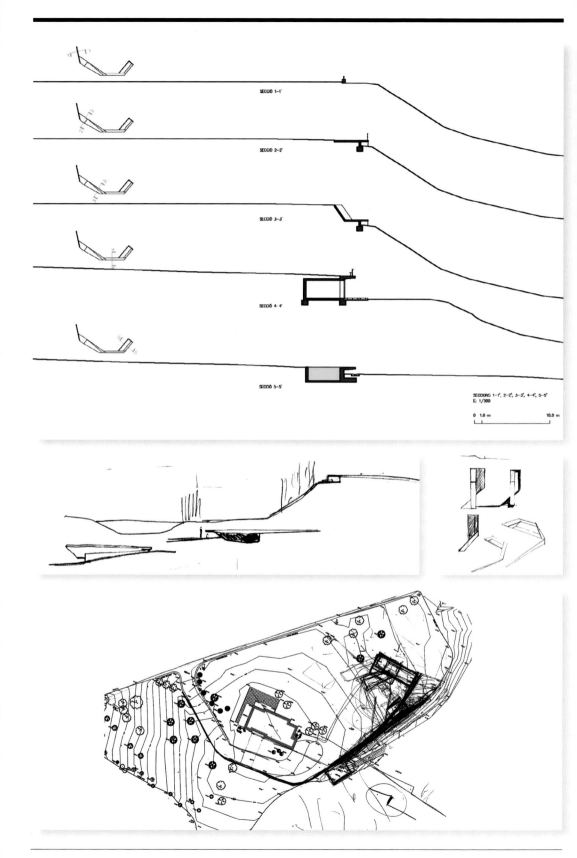

SECCIÓ 1-1'

SECCIÓ 2-2'

SECCIÓ 3-3'

SECCIÓ 4-4'

SECCIÓ 5-5'

SECCIONS 1-1', 2-2', 3-3', 4-4', 5-5'
E. 1/300

0   1,0 m   10,0 m

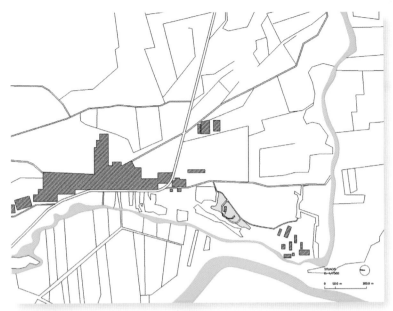

FLOODABLE GARDEN
Outdoor space for a single-family house (2004)

Location Calonge (Baix Empordà)
Clients Joaquim Ortega, Pilar Cerdà
Architects F451 Arquitectura | www.f451arquitectura.com
Toni Montes, Santi Ibarra, Lluís Ortega, Xavier Osarte, Esther Segura
Collaborating architect Ricardo Schultz
Project leader Toni Montes
Contractor Grieg Sounders
Budget € 36,340
Photography F451 Arquitectura

The preexisting situation is a small garden with terraces that has to accommodate a significant vertical drop. The biggest terrace is occupied almost entirely by a rectangular pool. The presence of this pool limits the use of the garden to the summer months, whereas the rest of the year it is empty and thus dangerous for small children. The commission is to eliminate the pool and take back this space for a play area.

Our proposal is based on the reformulation of the initial demand, with the objective of intensifying the use of this outside space as much as possible. We propose, on one hand, to provide versatility to the existing space depending on the different climatic conditions that can be predicted over the year. On the other hand, we wish to open up a series of different stages, to encourage the development of several activities and make them coexist simultaneously. The central design theme that arises from this approach is the conversion of part of the garden into a floodable garden, meaning that the space used as a play area in cold months becomes a pool in warm months.

The technique used is the reconfiguration of the existing topography on the basis of three conditions:
1. Keeping the more developed trees and bushes in their place.
2. Dissolving the system of terraces into a continuous topography that offers several alternatives of ascending paths.
3. Generating geometries that can retain up to 80 cm deep water basins.

The trees that must be conserved determine the fixed points of the geometry. Around them earth containers made of fiberglass are built, which serve to negotiate with the different topographic conditions. This procedure allows for the generation of heterogeneous topographical situations that are qualified specifically by the pavement: concrete in those areas that can contain water, wood on flat surfaces that serve as terraces, and green surfaces in those areas that work as transition points between the new topography and the immediate surroundings.

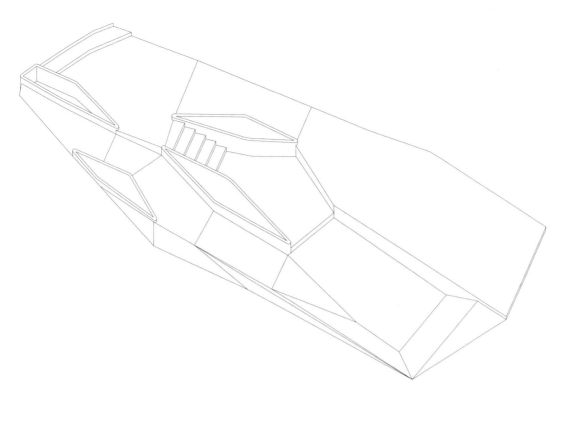

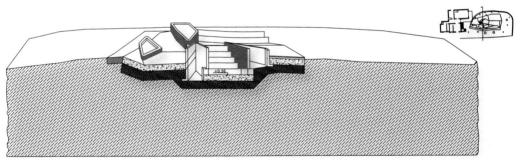

SECCION 4

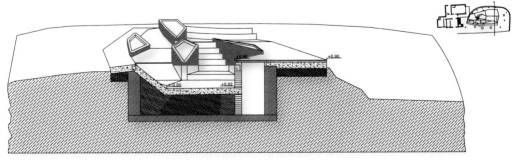

SECCION 5

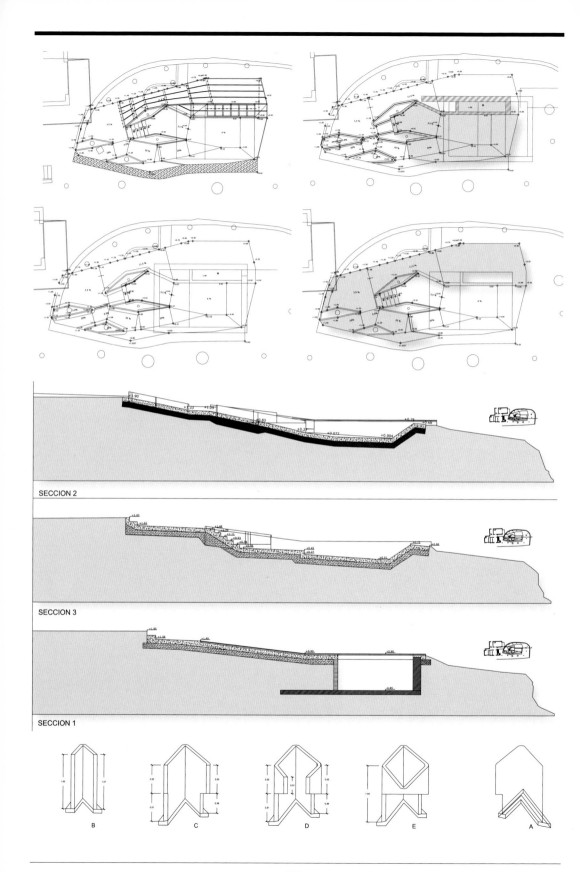

SECCION 2

SECCION 3

SECCION 1

B

C

D

E

A

PANORAMIC STAIRCASE
New entrance and façade for the Manresa town hall (2005-2008)

Location Manresa
Client Ayuntamiento de Manresa
Architects Manuel Bailo, Rosa Rull (ADD+arquitectura) | www.addarquitectura.net
Project leader Joan Maroto
Design team Albert Brito, Marc Camallonga, Natali Canas, Narcís Font, Mavi Hita, Jordi Palà, Anna Rovira, Maria Rull, Laurent Troost (ADD+arquitectura)
Structural engineering Martí Cabestany
M&E engineering Víctor Barnes
Technical architect Joel Vives
Photographs ADD+arquitectura

The town hall building is located at the edge of the plateau that is occupied by the old part of the city and looks over the river Cardener, facing the mountains of Montserrat. The main façade looks over the town square, acting as a conclusion of the different itineraries that cross the city's historic district. The back façade of the building is the limit we redefine. Here, the terrain drops quickly down to the river.

Working on a new staircase at the rear of the town hall building while simultaneously repairing its derelict façade allowed us to concentrate the tensions of this specific site in the design. This meant continuity with the old part and an open relationship with the landscape.

The staircase proposal can be seen as fragments of those itineraries that penetrate the building, extending towards the riverbanks as cantilevered balconies. A panoramic staircase, an intervention between land and city.

The staircase envelope is adjusted to the strictly used and necessary volume. It is not meant to be understood as a new closure added to an existing surface, but as a material continuation of the façade, adapted at times to occasional geometries.

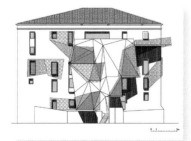

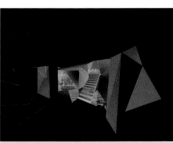

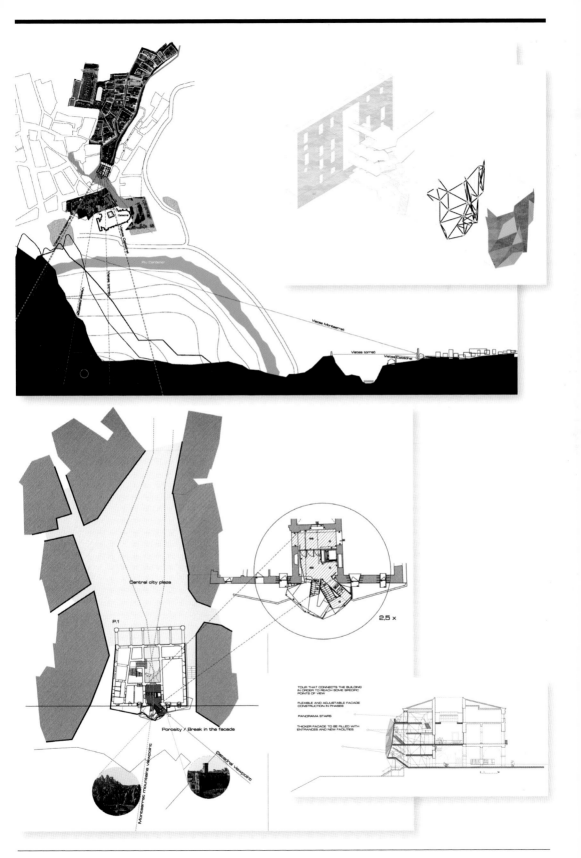

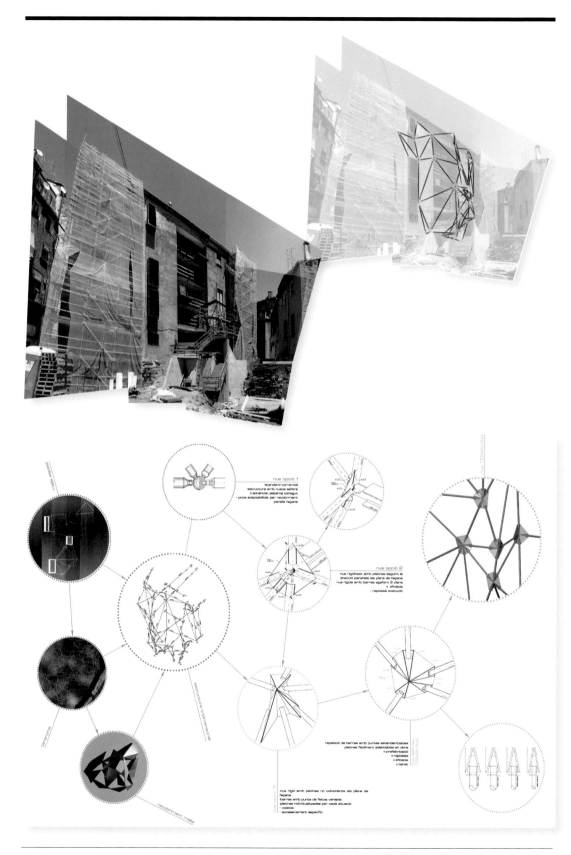

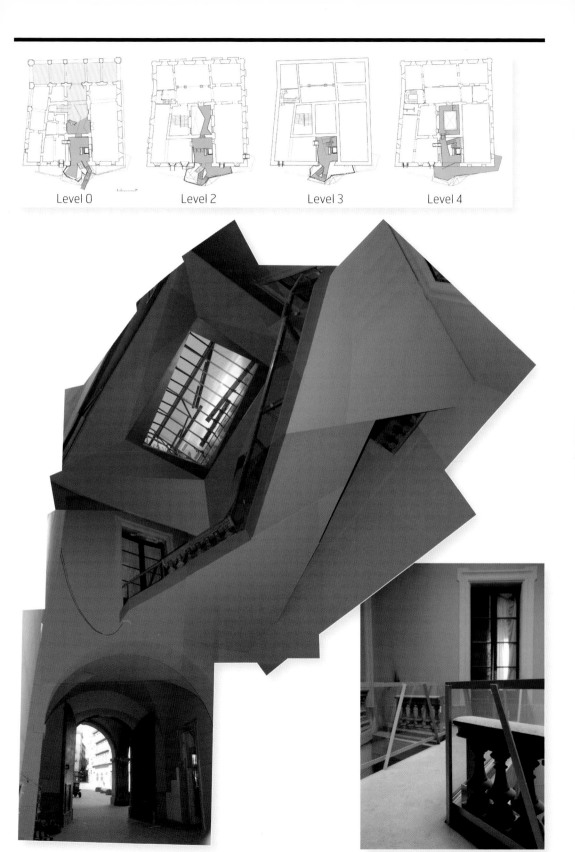

Level 0   Level 2   Level 3   Level 4

FRACTAL PLATFORMS
Reorganisation of a bathing area (2006)

Location Vinaròs
Client Ajuntament de Vinaròs, Generalitat Valenciana, Ministerio de Turismo
Architects Why Art Projects: Vicente Guallart, María Díaz, Christine Bleitcher
www.guallart.com
Geometry consultant Marta Malé
Site architect Vicente Guallart
Budget € 600,000
Photographs Laura Cantarella, Why Art Projects

In 1967 Benoit Mandelbrot published his famous text "How long is the coast of Britain?" in *Science* magazine. This text and his subsequent book, *The fractal Geometry*, were the origin of a whole new line of research on the geometry of irregular systems. The coast, the line that separates the land from water, is one of those systems.

In Vinaròs, a city of 30,000, the regional government, la Generalitat Valenciana, is promoting the reorganization of the port. The industrial and fishing areas will be extended and moved to the south dyke, and a new marina will be built in conjunction with the extension of the promenade.

A rocky area is located to the south of the port. It has a natural beach where a rain water sewer flows into the sea. An hexagonal pattern was devised for the renovation of the beach, which operates by creating various interior and exterior coastline extensions to the rocky perimeter, with different functions and materials.

A restaurant is built halfway between the water edge and the upper level, at a point that allows one to reconstruct the original coastline at a lower resolution than the original. The beach is organized at a higher resolution by means of a huge cement boomerang that holds the sewer underneath and creates a "beach on the beach."

An artificial wooden island, placed next to the sea in the summer and next to the restaurant in the winter, promotes a dynamic transformation of the coastline.

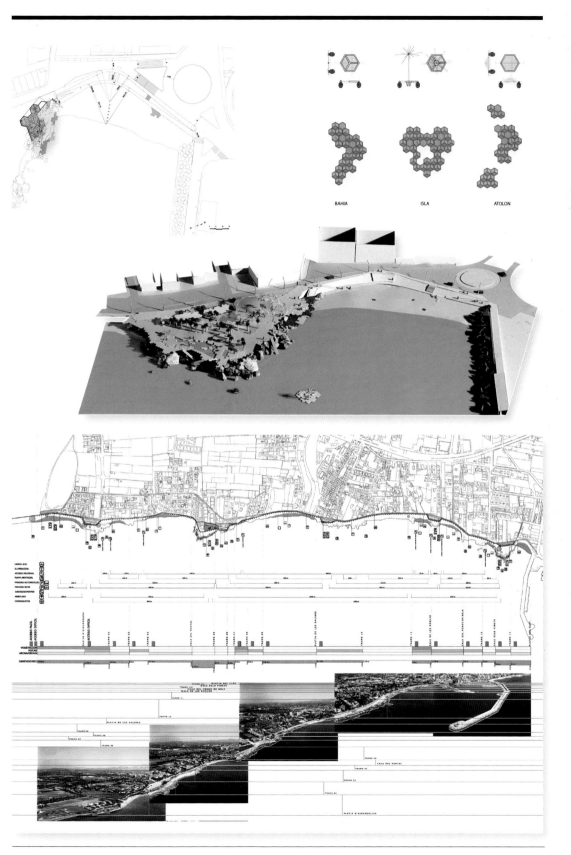

BAHIA   ISLA   ATOLON

URBAN CLERESTORY
Noise reduction barriers (1999-2006)

Location Av. Gran Via de les Corts Catalanes, Barcelona
Client Ajuntament de Barcelona, Generalitat de Catalunya IMU-BIMSA
Architects EMBT Arquitectes Associats (Enric Miralles, Benedetta Tagliabue)
www.mirallestagliabue.com
Achitect on site Joan Callís
Project leaders Makoto Fukuda, Lluís Corbella
Design team Peter Sándor Nagy, Joan Callís
Acoustics Higini Arau
Structural engineering MC2. Julio Martínez Calzón
Models Christian Molina, Abelardo Gómez, Miguel Sánchez, Felipe Bernal,
Miguel Andrés Sánchez, Catalina Pinzón
Photography Duccio Malagamba, EMBT

The definition of this section of Gran Via in the form of a trench is based on the radical separation between car traffic and pedestrians, creating a topography for rapid circulation. But this is an avenue with an urban vocation, almost with the ambition to be a park. The objective of our intervention is to reduce the perception of intense traffic from the higher levels of adjacent buildings and from public space.
The acoustic screens are located on the edges of side slabs that form the trench section, built five meters above the sunk traffic lanes. The screen is a rigid element formed by a resistant outer skin that envelops a softer core of low density acoustic material. The enveloping surfaces are are concave on the part that is exposed to the noise and flat on the other side. As a whole, it makes up a structure that is 2.5 meters high, with a varying thickness between 10 and 50 cm.

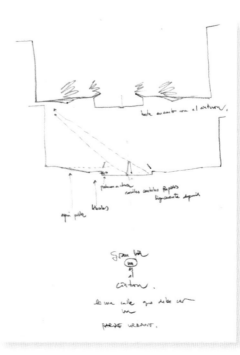

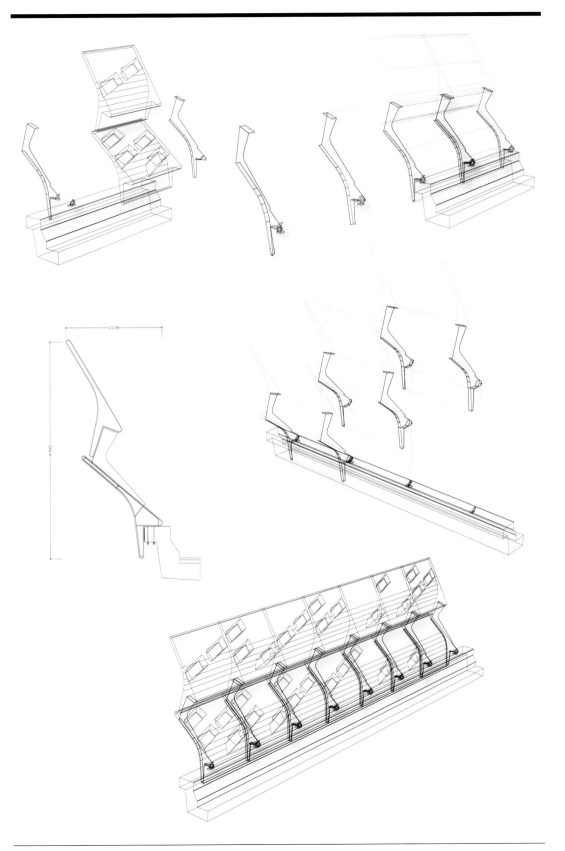

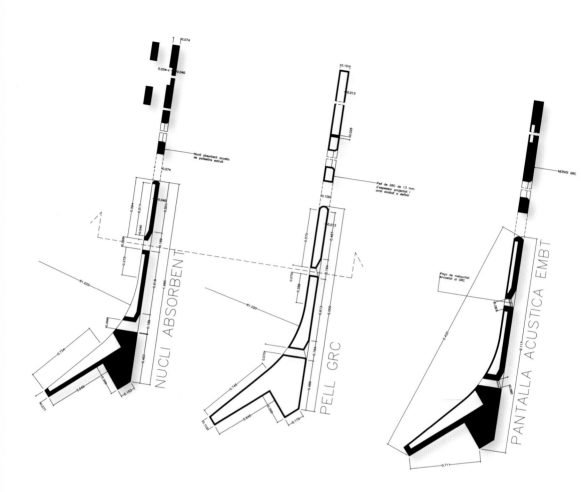

NUCLI ABSORBENT

PELL GRC

PANTALLA ACUSTICA EMBT

Nucli absorbent acústic de poliestirè extruït

Pell de GRC de 13 mm d'espessor projectat, i amb acabat a definir

NERVIS GRC

Peça de metacrilat encastat al GRC

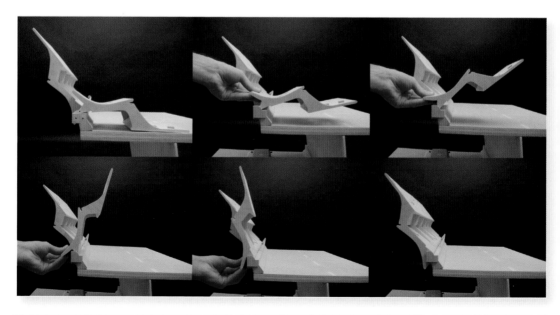

PHOTOVOLTAIC CANOPY
Forum 2004 esplanade (2001-2004)

Location Barcelona
Client Infrastructures del Llevant
Architects Martínez Lapeña-Torres Arquitectos, S.L., José Antonio Martínez Lapeña, Elías Torres Tur
Engineer Esteyco Consultor, Javier Rui-Wamba (Civil engineer)
Collaborators Esteyco Consultor-Ingeniería: Andreu Estany, Ricardo Gil, Carlos García, Miguel Ángel Fernández / Martínez Lapeña-Torres Architects: Aurora Armental, Pau Badia, Josep Ballestero, Guillem Bosch, Marta Carbonell, Alexandra de Châtillon, Luigi Dall'Argine, Daniela Eckardt, Sylvia Felipe, Emilia Fossati, Pau Fulleda, Marc García-Durán, Borja José Gutiérrez, Laura Jiménez, Majbritt Lerche, Iago López, Lluisa Morao Igesias, José Manuel Navarro, Estanislao Puig, Fidel Savall Sargas, Pablo Tena, Luis Valiente, Jennifer Vera
Contractors Drace/Dragados/Copcisa, Necso/Rubau, ACS/Necso, Preufet, Six Constructors
Subcontractors Hormipresa, Caldesa, Bega/Carandini, Escofet, Prefabricados Castelo, Ursa, Isofotón, Sener, Inabensa
Photography Elías Torres, Estudio Martínez Lapeña - Torres, Aviotec

The Forum esplanade, a support for the Forum building and the new Convention Centre (CCIB), shaped like an open hand or a delta, is a 14 hectare extension of the Diagonal avenue that covers a large part of the newly extended water treatment plant. This roof can be seen as a cloth, an image that the asphalt pavement—a huge 5 colour patchwork—refers to quite explicitly. A pavement that is also a complex technical floor under which power lines, water pipes, telephone lines and a drainage system form a dense network. The future uses will imply unforeseeable occupations of this esplanade.

Over this esplanade emerge chimneys and services of the water treatment plant, as well as two folded canopies that have been built to provide shade and two large hypostyle halls—the structure of which is coincident with that of the underlying water tanks on which it rests. These two large concrete canopies, which are open on all four sides, will hold a metallic shed structure (whose north face will be glazed and whose south side will be covered with 6.500 m² of photovoltaic cell panels) that will provide a 13.000 m² roof for the esplanade.

The *fingers* of the esplanade rise in such a way that they form a series of *cliffs* over the new marina, while the interstices among them house ramps and stairs that allow people to descend to the port. The two fingers located closest to the sea house a dry marina and a sailing school that holds a large photovoltaic canopy (4.500 m²). This canopy will be seen in Barcelona's waterfront as yet another of the industrial facilities that are so characteristic of this area.

The canopy receives sunlight and produces energy and a cane-like shadow. It is a skewed plane, with a 30° inclination and oriented due south, supported by 4 twisted legs that stick out of the Sailing School finger. The roof of this building is a geometrically unexpected end to the Diagonal avenue, the last view-point or belvedere of the city over the water which can finally be reached descending a large staircase *"under a pallium"*.

esplanada 2004.
11·12·2003·

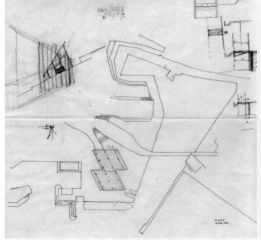

PLANTA GENERAL

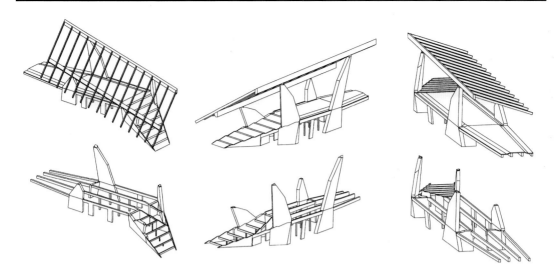

GARDEN OVER THE HORTA BUS DEPOT, BARCELONA

Jaime Coll (JC), Coll-Leclerc Arquitectes
Judith Leclerc (JL), Coll-Leclerc Arquitectes
Teresa Galí (TG), agronomic engineer

JL In our competition entry for the bus depot of the Transports Metropolitans de Barcelona (TMB), located between the Ronda de Dalt (the city's ring road) and the hills of Collserola, we had thought of a roof slab divided into four flat, staggered platforms, each characterized by a type of planting and usage. In the end, the building project was assigned to other architects, who proposed building a green covering, divided into different sections with thyme bushes and other aromatic plants. We, however, were finally commissioned to create the park on this roof designed by the other firm. First we had to decide how to guarantee the proper draining of a 20,000 m² decking where only two large gutters on two sides had been planned, and at the same time how to control the soil to avoid it being carried away by rain water. Another condition was the weight that the roof could hold, which limited the soil depth to one meter.

TG We couldn't apply here green roofing techniques typical in other areas of Europe since, in our climate, autumn storms can be produce large quantities of water in little time. We had to refer to the experience of the sewer system of the city of Barcelona, with one gutter planned for every 200 to 400 m² to ensure the collection and evacuation of water in a quick and controlled manner. The project was thus based on several limitations: the need to fragment the surface of the roof to allow the evacuation of rain water, the load limit of the structure, the topography of the base (the geometry of the roof), and regulations that required us to use drain pipes with a minimum diameter of 400 mm, the standard pipe size of public sewers. For all of these reasons, we had to build our topography with a light and flexible system. We studied some past projects, especially the paving stones of the Rambla del Brasil, by Olga Tarrasó and Jordi Henrich, built over a part of the Ronda del Mig in Barcelona. There a topography had been constructed with a base of expanded clay, which is a material with no consistency and no containing capacity, which brought about many problems in the construction process. We then decided to speak to Antonio Casado, owner of Acycsa, who proposed different solutions.

JC In a brainstorming session we had with him in 2001, several solutions came up for the different problems that we had: lightening the structure, holding soil, channelling water, etc. In fact, the main problem that we had was the load. We had to calculate the permanent weight of the soil and vegetation (which was 1000 kg/m²), and the overload of use, conditioned by the type of trucks that would access that roof. The maintenance of a landscaped surface of 2 hectares inevitably required an access for trucks. Another paradox existed, an item incompatibility, which was the structural grid of 14 m x 14 m that is required by a bus depot. Those large spans are usually incompatible with the occupation of the roof as a public space. The structure of a conventional parking ramp, with structural grids of 5 x 7.5 m or 7.5 x 7.5 m and a 50 cm thick slab, could have held up a layer of 1.5 m of earth. But in this case, with a meter-thick roof and another meter of soil to define the topography, we could not place enough soil to guarantee the successful growth of the type of plants we had imagined and we had too much weight for the structural spans we were standing on.

JL The issue was how to find a material or a construction system that was flexible enough to contain the topography that we wanted to produce without having to repeat the matrix of the base that held us up. We didn't want the checkered geometry of the floor slabs to determine the geometry of the park.

JC   Casado proposed using cardboard with wires as a good solution to form light structures. At that time, we thought of experiences like the *Endless House* of Frederick Kiesler, as a way of creating vaults with light material, but we soon ruled that idea out. We also thought of the use of inflatables which would act as a lost formwork.

JL   But the problem in this case was how to control the geometry, that here would become much more random.

JC   Casado also spoke of using the typical one meter-cubed sacks used for construction site debris filled with expanded clay. But waterproofing was still left to figure out, and since it was a system that was not standardized or approved, we had to rule that idea out. Besides, there was also the budget issue; expanded clay is an expensive material and we would have needed 20,000 sacks of it. Then Casado proposed using residual mud from water treatment plants as a filling material but we had to make sure that it didn't get wet, otherwise it would contaminate the area. In this case, the material that would inflate the structure would not be air, but a light material, a recycled product.

TG   Now I am testing this technique with the architects Batlle i Roig, in the project of La Vall d'en Joan, in the old landfill of El Garraf. Among the products that reach waste treatment plants, those with a low percentage of organic material are selected and wrapped in plastic film, from which large, compact, insulated, and water-tight bales made of waste material are obtained to serve as filling. With no air or light, leaching does not occur and biological processes are not produced on the inside. It is a material that is stable and inert, as well as stackable. We are now verifying its resistence.

JL   Casado saw that we were a little obsessed with the shape, with the geometry of the project. The proposals that he had made were all rather formless and we didn't know if we would end up having to build walls in order to organize the filling material. Then he proposed that we build our topography using plastic caissons, the elements used as molds in the construction of some concrete floor slabs. What we thought of was the possibility of stacking these elements and thus going past the meter thickness that we achieved with normal soil. Using two levels of 70 cm caissons and one meter of lightened soil, we could obtain thicknesses of almost 2.5 meters. Since the caissons are very small elements, we could control the geometry more freely and precisely, and also with more freedom in regards to the geometry of the base, without showing what was underneath. TMB asked us for a technical study to demonstrate that the caissons were resistent and stackable enough without large deformations in the 20,000 m² of park. We had to make a computerized model of the deformation estimate and we demostrated that a slab of 7 x 7 meters was only deformed by 2 mm per side, acceptable in this type of structure.

The first step was the building of the drains. In the sequence of aerial photos, the platforms defined by the given roof are easily seen as is the placement of the sewer pipes on top of them. Afterwards, the small black pieces of the caissons were placed by area and were gradually covered with a stabililzing layer of concrete. The new geometry of the surface defines funnels that act as retaining walls in case the caissons were to move and at the same time allow for the soil to be retained. This is how we ended up doing the substructure of the topography.

JC　　We went from those first proposals that allowed us little control over the shape to a more rigid material and at the same time smaller, a more controllable size. From the 1 x 1 meter size of the sacks we went to the 50 x 50 cm surface of the caisson. On the other hand, the sealing and covering with a stabilizing concrete layer make this caisson construction behave like a vault in a resource remniscent of the structure of Park Güell, with its sand-filled brick vaults.

TG　　At some point in fact we thought we could also reproduce the drainage system used in Park Güell, perforating the roof and draining through the columns that support it. If we had been able to bring each of these funnels all the way to the ground and go directly through the roof, we would have saved a lot of infrastructure and a lot of money. But the roof slab that we were given was not perforable, so we could only drain on the edges. I think this was the only possible solution to evacuate the water well in those conditions. The topography forms two basins that collect water in two deposits (these disappeared in the management process) that would have provided water for irrigation.

JC　　Once we decided that this artificial, hollowed-out topography, with a network of gutters of the sufficient dimensions for water collection would work, we came closer to the more conceptual point of the project, its formal definition. As a base, we used Giacometti's horizontal sculptures and game boards from the late 1920s and early 1930s. We were interested in the process of abstraction that Giacometti followed with African masks, turning the face into a landscape. The frontal view became the aerial view. This is related to our topography in the sense that the proportion between surface and height is inverted, little height for extended length and width. Giacometti's sculpture *No more play* (*On ne joue plus*, 1932) was basic for our project because it allowed us to understand movement and the different speeds of park users: the car, the bicycle, the pedestrian, skates, dogs, etc. From that reflection, we decided on the materials that would cover the funnels (hard or soft, warm or cool), to later choose the vegetation and determine what activities would be possible on each one: picnicking, children's games, "toilets" for dogs, fountains, etc. The fact that the funnels are circular generates residual space between them and it may have been possible to build a similar organization with a deformable polygonal geometry. But we were interested in the circular geometry of the funnels to separate the spaces of activity and the residual gaps between them to define rough spaces.

TG　　In fact, our work in this park could have ended here: with the definition of a roof that collects waters, located on the urban limit of the Collserola hills that define the city's edge. Over time, the mountain's vegetation would have invaded the park and would have been distributed according to the different characteristics of the areas that we had invented. It would have been nice to see how that colonization of nature would have taken place.

JL　　But the idea for a park arised as a demand from the neighbors, and the uses and circulations that they proposed conditioned the control over elevation, slopes, and plants. In the end an area of two hectares was recovered by residents; this is a good thing.

JC　　This also has to do with an intelligent political decision, recovering in the form of a park the land that a large infrastructure is to be built on. In fact, the area between the city's ring road and the hills is full of large facilities (hospital, velodrome, morgue, etc.). It is interesting to see how limits that are so clearly defined on the map from an urban planning point of view have to adapt to the reality of the orography of the location, much more devious and complex. What is clear is that the depot was located on an underpinning of the mountain and could become the trampoline from which the vegetation of Collserola bounces off into the city.

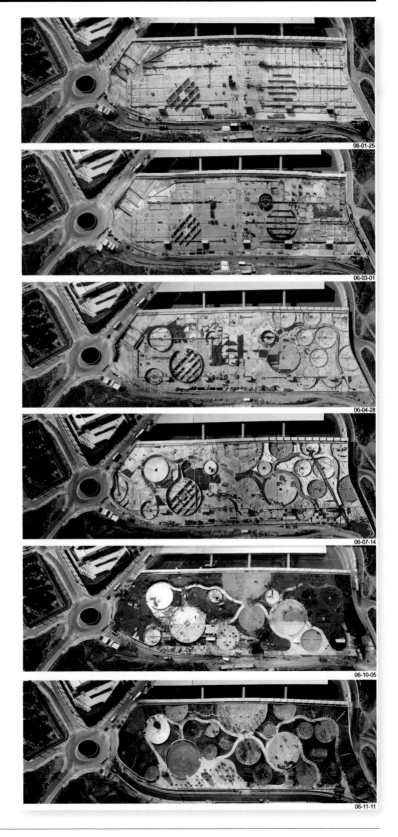

06-01-25

06-03-01

06-04-28

06-07-14

06-10-05

06-11-11

HYPOSTYLE GARDEN
Park on a bus depot (2002-2006)

Location Horta, Barcelona
Client TMB - Transports de Barcelona SA / Barcelona Regional
Architects Jaime Coll, Judith Leclerc | www.coll-leclerc.com
Landscape architect Teresa Galí
Structural consultants David Garcia, Bis arquitectes
Engineering Manel Comas
Technical architect Xavier Badia
Design team Adrià Goula, Jordi Giralt, Tomeu Ramis, Alberto Sánchez, Narcís Font, Cristian Vivas, José Ulloa
Contractor COMSA
Project management GRECCAT, Josep Miquel Riba
Budget € 4,276,669
Photographs José Hevia

The intervention on the deck of the Horta depot sets off from two principles:

1. Provide the deck of the bus depot of the Transports Metropolitans de Barcelona at Horta with a park and facilities that work as a future gate to the park of Collserola.

2. Guarantee a proper water drainage, very important on a 20,000 m^2 roof

The park is thus presented as a large drainage and water pipe machine, which separates water into superficial flows and then into deeper drains. The artificiality of the location, a park on a roof at the limits of an urban area, is reflected in funnels (superficial waters) while its more natural aspect is expressed on the rough areas between funnels (deep waters).

The large concrete funnels collect torrential rain water towards a large central gutter. They are areas free of vegetation, basins with various finishing materials that generate two types of landscape: a cool landscape (sand, water, marble edges, ivy, and concrete) or a warm landscape (grass, climbing plants, colored rubber). The cool landscape will produce dynamic activity (skating, playing in the water, trial bike, remote controlled cars, children's games), while the warm landscape will produce reposed activity (stretching, sunbathing, reading, rolling around, picnicking, gardening).

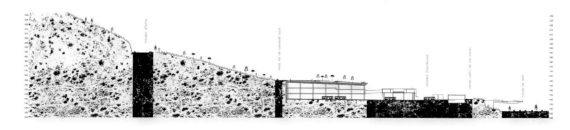

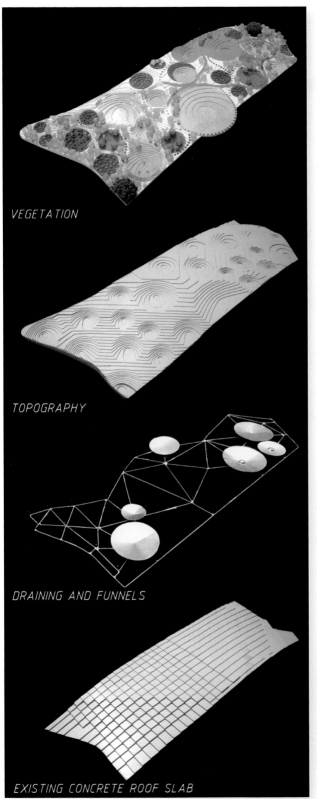

VEGETATION

TOPOGRAPHY

DRAINING AND FUNNELS

EXISTING CONCRETE ROOF SLAB

ESQUEMA DE EVACUACIÓN DE LAS AGUAS: SISTEMA DE
TRIPLE IMPERMEABILIZACIÓN

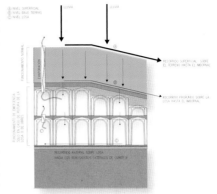

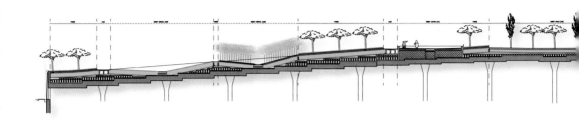

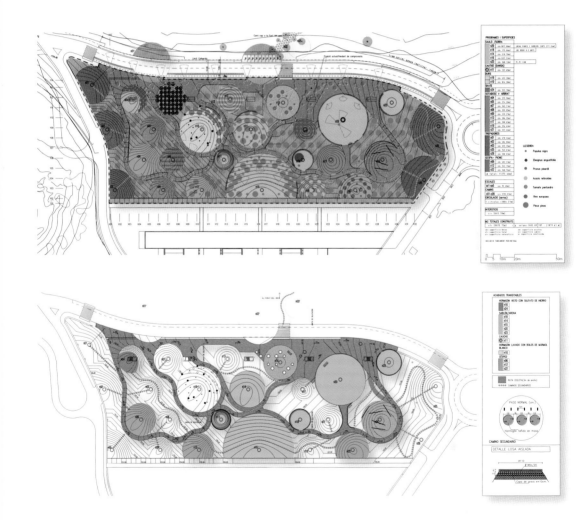

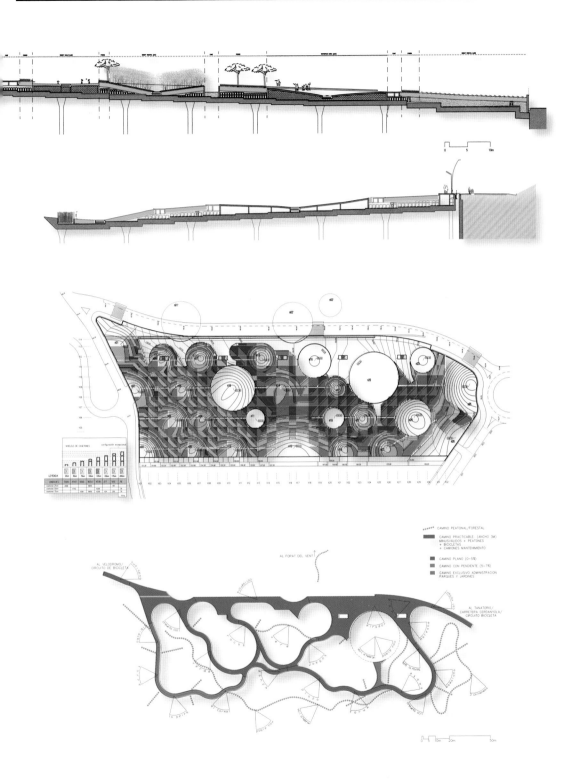

#01 #10 #19

#02 #11 #20

#03 #12 #21

#04 #13 #22

#05 #14 #23

#06 #15 #24

#07 #16 #25

#08 #17 #26

#09 #18

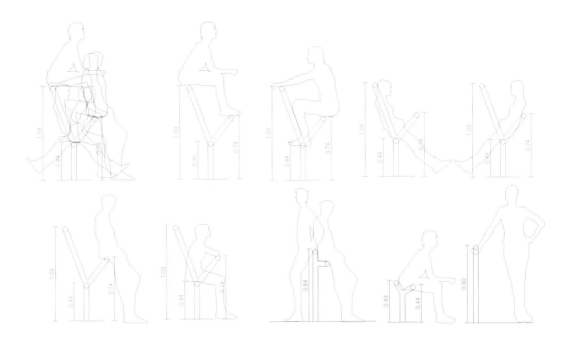

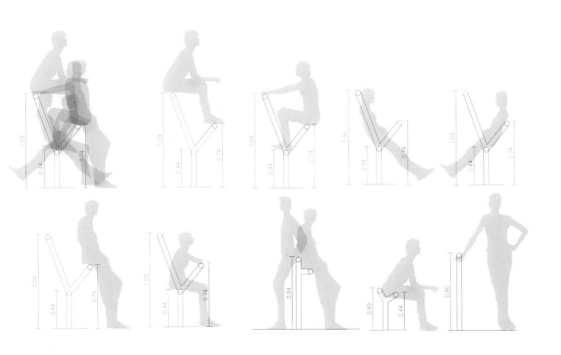

This catalogue is published on occasion of the exhibition organised by the Ramon Llull Institute and the Deutsches Architekturmuseum, presented in Frankfurt from 14th September to 18th November 2007, to mark the 2007 edition of the Frankfurt Book Fair at which Catalan culture is the Guest of Honour.

EHRENGAST / GUEST OF HONOUR
CULTURA CATALANA
SINGULAR i UNIVERSAL
FRANKFURTER BUCHMESSE 2007
FRANKFURT BOOK FAIR 2007

10-14 October 2007
FRANKFURTER BUCHMESSE
Guest of Honour >Catalan Culture<

Publishers

ACTAR
Barcelona / New York
info@actar.com
www.actar.com

Ramon Llull Institute
Barcelona
www.llull.cat

Deutsches Architekturmuseum
Frankfurt am Main
www.dam-online.de

Distribution

ACTAR D
Roca i Batlle 2
08023 Barcelona
T +34 93 4174993
F +34 93 4186707
office@actar-d.com
www.actar-d.com

Distribution USA

Actar Distribution Inc
159 Lafayette St. 5th Floor
New York, NY 10013
T +1 212 966 2207
F +1 212 966 2214
officeusa@actar-d.com
www.actar-d.com

ISBN: 978-84-96954-09-0
D.L.: B-39561-07
Printed and bound in the European Union

Grup Agbar

FUNDACIÓ CAIXA CATALUNYA

SanMiguel

VITICULTORS
Mas d'en Gil
PRIORAT

DELICATESSEN DEL PORC
Salgot

clickair
vola inteHigent

Ramon Llull Institute

Director Josep Bargalló
Assistant Director Neus Fornells
Planning and Communication Director Antoni Batista
Head of the Language Department Àngels Prats
Head of the Creation Department Borja Sitjà
Head of the Humanities and Science Department Carles Torner
Manager Josep Marcé
Frankfurt 2007 Project Organiser Anna Soler-Pont

Exhibition

Based on an original idea by Peter Cachola Schmal
Exhibition curators and designers Albert Ferré, Jaime Salazar, Ricardo Devesa
Graphic Design Christian Schärmer
Identity Ramon Prat
Administration and Management Inka Plechaty, Jeanette Bolz, Julia Nicolai, DAM
Production supervision Dolors Soriano, Leandre Linares
Printing Marc Martí
Steel structure Esteve Miret
Transport supervision Eulàlia Prat
Exhibition mounting Christian Walter, Marina Barry, Paolo Brunino, Enrico Hirsekorn, Eike Laeuen, Beate Voigt, Detlef Wagner-Walter, Herbert Warmuth, Gerhard Winkler, Valerian Wolenik

Catalogue

Editor Albert Ferré
with Anna Tetas and Ricardo Devesa
Graphic Design Christian Schärmer
Cover design Ramon Prat
Translations Wesley Trobaugh, Ted Krasny
Transcriptions Jordi Mallol
Production coordination Dolors Soriano, Leandre Linares
Printing Ingoprint

Acknowledgements

Fernando Marzá, Manel Parés, Olga Egea, Gemma Ferré, Marta Poch, Sílvia Canals, Miguel Carreiro, Albert Brito, Esther Rodríguez, Ricard Giró, Philipp Oswalt, Sonsoles Cerviño, Britta Gahmann, Isabel Delgado and Carlos Ipser.
The editors especially thank Peter Cachola Schmal and Annette Becker of the Deutsches Architekturmuseum for their initiative and support in the organisation of the exhibition.
The exhibition and this book would not have been possible without the help of the participating architecture offices.